Making
Wooden Toys

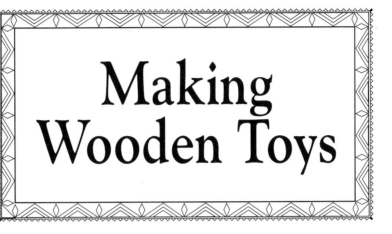

Making
Wooden Toys

Geoff Rugless

MILNER CRAFT SERIES

Disclaimer

The information in this instruction book is presented in good faith. However, no warranty is given, nor results guaranteed, nor is freedom from any patent to be inferred. Since we have no control over the information contained in this book, the publisher and the author disclaim liability for untoward results.

First published in 2000 by
Sally Milner Publishing Pty Ltd
734 Woodville Road
Binda NSW 2583 AUSTRALIA

© Geoff Rugless 2000
Reprinted 2010

Design by Anna Warren, Warren Ventures, Sydney
Photography by Geoff Rugless
Editing by Lyneve Rappell

Printed in Hong Kong

National Library of Australia Cataloguing-in-Publication data:

Rugless, Geoff.
Making wooden toys

ISBN 1 86351 246 2

Contents

Introduction

The toys in this book have been designed with three goals in mind.

- To be attractive to children and fun to play with.
- To be simple, inexpensive and a pleasure to make.
- To be safe.

CUTTING LIST

Each project begins with a Cutting List. This has been designed to help you purchase the required amounts of pine. However, most stores sell pine by the metre so it works out more economical if you make several projects together.

MATERIALS

I have selected pine as the basic material because it is budget-friendly and easy to work with. Shapes have been kept simple. The toys are constructed using standard sizes of pine that can be purchased from most hardware stores.

ALL PROJECTS REQUIRE:
- PVA glue
- Drawing pencil
- Bullet head nails or Brads (sizes listed per project)
- Wood filler (pine coloured if using clear paint)
- 80-100 grit sandpaper

SOME PROJECTS ALSO REQUIRE:
- 4 mm plywood
- Square and half-round moulding (various sizes, see projects)
- Scotia (cornice)
- Dowelling, various sizes ranging from 6 mm to 16 mm
- Flat head nails
- 6 mm screw eyes
- Hinges
- Various screws and washers

EQUIPMENT

You won't need elaborate or expensive tools. The tools you will need are already in most home workshops:

- Power drill with bits ranging from 1.5 to 10 mm. A drill press is a great advantage for lining up holes.
- Power jigsaw, fretsaw or tenon saw
- Keyhole saw
- Hammer (small tack hammer is best for these projects)
- Nail punch
- 25 mm (1") spade bit
- Hole saws (usually come in a set)
- 50 mm (2") hole saw (usually purchased separately)
- Vise and clamps
- Plane
- Rasp

TIPS FOR USING TOOLS

- Always follow the manufacturers safety instructions that come with your tools.
- Purchase good quality hole saws and a good spade bit. Keep the spade bit sharp.
- Take care when using a spade bit. Make sure the wood is securely clamped and, if you have one, a drill press will help hold the drill steady. A spade bit can also leave a jagged edge on the reverse side of the wood. To avoid this, drill most of the way through the piece then remove the bit from the hole and turn the wood over. Realign the drill and finish cutting.

PAINT

The toys will look better and last longer if they are painted. Nearly all paints these days are lead/toxin free, but you should inquire anyway. Gloss paint enamel makes an attractive toy but the wood will need to be sealed with undercoat or sealer first. Water-based clear matt or gloss paint will enhance the natural appearance of the toys and doesn't need undercoating.

Warning

Toys that are being built for children three years and under should not be nailed. In most cases, glue will serve to secure the parts. If you feel a more secure attachment is required, use 6 mm dowelling glued into pre-drilled 6 mm holes in the corresponding parts.

Cradle

CUTTING LIST

Pine
450 x 120 x 12 mm — headboard, footboard,
two rockers, floor

4 mm plywood
179 x 57 mm — sides

MATERIALS
12 mm bullet head nails
20 mm bullet head nails
25 mm flat head nails

EQUIPMENT
19 mm hole saw or spade bit
Keyhole saw
Rasp

INSTRUCTIONS

1. Read through all the instructions. Check the template and assembly chart and photograph before beginning the project. Use a photocopier to enlarge the template to full size. Trace the template diagrams onto the pieces of wood listed in the cutting list.
2. Using the jigsaw or fretsaw, cut out the headboard, footboard, floor and rockers.

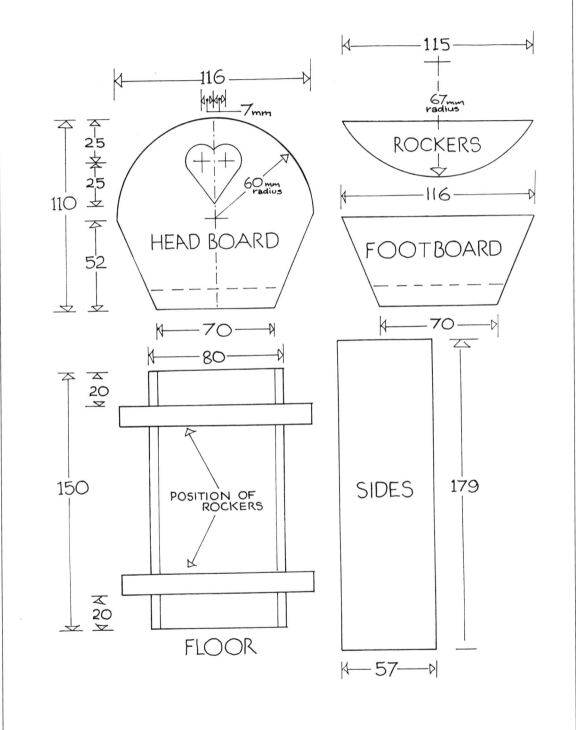

116

7mm

25

25

110

52

60mm radius

HEAD BOARD

70

115

67mm radius

ROCKERS

116

FOOTBOARD

70

80

20

150

POSITION OF ROCKERS

20

FLOOR

SIDES

179

57

3. Cut out the heart-shape on the headboard by using a 19 mm hole saw or spade bit to shape the curved tops and finishing the straight sides with the jigsaw or a keyhole saw.

4. Cut out the floor. Using a rasp and sandpaper, bevel the side edges to match the angle of the sides of the headboard and footboard.

5. Glue and nail the headboard to one end of the floor. Glue and nail the footboard to the other end the floor. Use 20 mm bullet head nails.

6. Cut out the cradle sides. Glue and nail the sides to the headboard, footboard and floor using 12 mm bullet head nails.

7. Cut out the rockers. Using the template as a guide, glue and nail them to the underside of the floor using 25 mm flat head nails.

8. Paint the cradle. You may wish to decorate the cradle using stencils, as shown in the photograph.

Car

CUTTING LIST

Pine
176 x 90 x 35 mm — body
316 x 70 x 19 mm — wheels and mudguards

4 mm plywood
52 x 73 mm — running board

6 mm dowelling
Two 78 mm lengths — axles

MATERIALS
15 mm bullet head nails
25 mm bullet head nails

EQUIPMENT
50 mm hole saw
7 mm drill bit
25 mm spade bit

INSTRUCTIONS

1. Read through all the instructions. Check the template and assembly chart and photograph before beginning the project. Use a photocopier to enlarge the template to full size. Trace the template diagrams onto the pieces of wood listed in the cutting list.
2. Cut out the body.

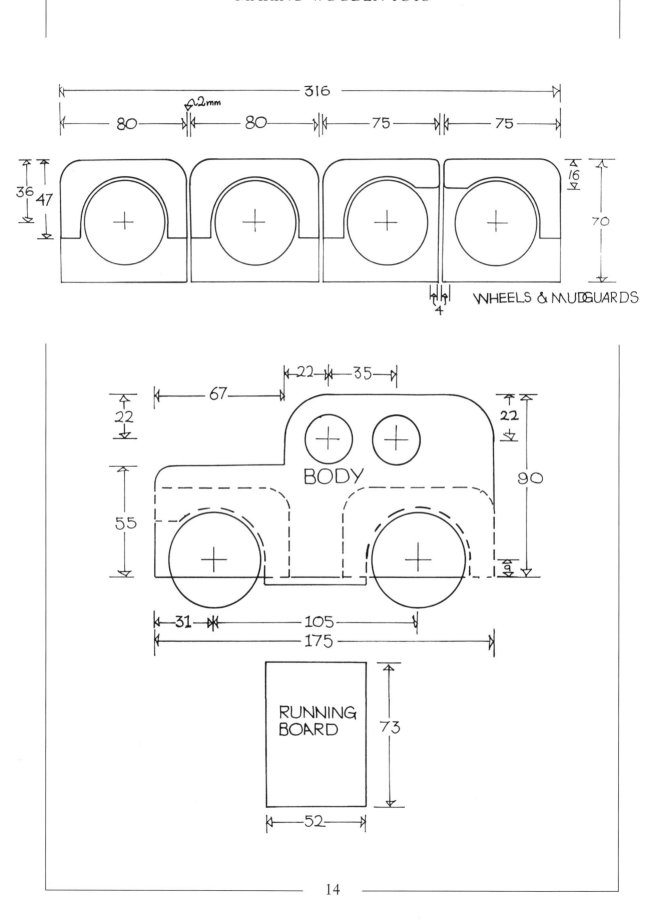

WHEELS & MUDGUARDS

BODY

RUNNING
BOARD

3. Using a 25 mm spade bit, drill the two window holes.

4. Drill two 7 mm axle holes in the positions marked on the template.

5. Using a 50 mm hole saw, cut the four wheels out of the pine block (DO NOT cut the pine block into sections first). The wheels will have a 6 mm hole in the centre for attaching to the axles in step 10.

6. Using a jigsaw or tenon saw, cut the pine block into sections, as marked on the template. Trim the pieces to create the mudguards. Round off the edges using sandpaper.

7. Positioning the mudguards correctly is important to prevent the wheels rubbing on them. Do this by first putting one of the axles through one of the wheels. Temporarily position the axle in an axle hole. Pre-drill two fine pilot holes in the mudguard to prevent the wood from splitting when nailed. Line up the mudguard to fit around the wheel without touching it. Glue and nail the mudguard into position. Use 25 mm bullet head nails and punch the heads below the surface. Remove the wheel and axle. Repeat the procedure for the remaining wheels. Fill the holes with wood filler and sand off all sharp edges.

8. Cut out the running board. Glue and nail it to the base of the car using 15 mm bullet heads.

9. Paint the body and wheels separately using a non-toxic gloss paint.

10. When the paint is dry, pass the dowelling axles through the axle holes in the body. Then, glue the wheels to the axles.

Bus

CUTTING LIST

Pine
242 x 90 x 35 mm — body
316 x 70 x 19 mm — wheels and mudguards

4 mm plywood
55 x 73 mm — running board

6 mm dowelling
Two 78 mm lengths — axles

MATERIALS
25 mm bullet head nails
12 mm bullet head nails

EQUIPMENT
50 mm hole saw
7 mm drill bit
25 mm spade bit

INSTRUCTIONS

1. Read through all the instructions. Check the template, assembly chart and photograph before beginning the project. Use a photocopier to enlarge the template to full size. Trace the template diagrams onto the pieces of wood listed in the cutting list.
2. Cut out the body.

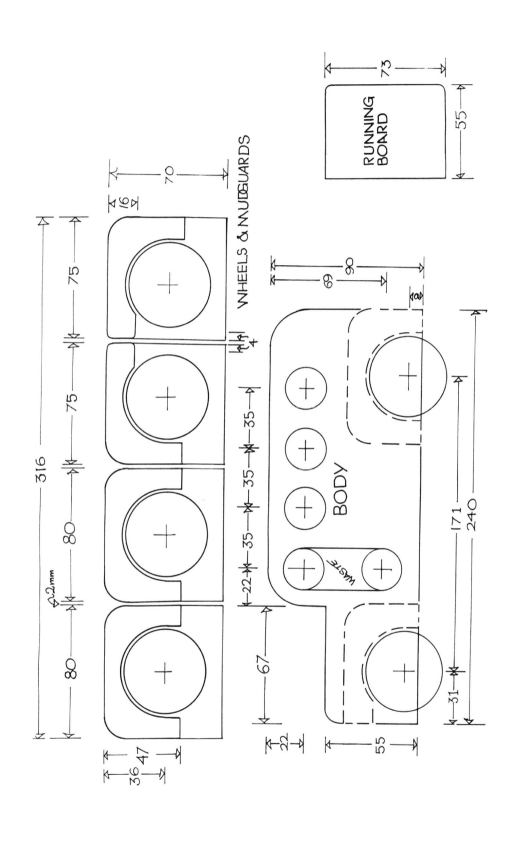

RUNNING BOARD

WHEELS & MUDGUARDS

BODY

WASTE

3. Using a 25 mm spade bit, drill five holes in the body for the door and windows, in positions marked on template. Using a key hole saw, cut out the waste between the two front holes to make the door.

4. Drill two 7 mm axle holes in the positions marked on the template.

5. Using a 50 mm hole saw to cut out the four wheels. The wheels will have a 6 mm hole in the centre for attaching the axles in step 10.

6. Using a jigsaw, cut out the mudguards, as shown on template.

7. Positioning the mudguards correctly is important to prevent the wheels from binding. First, put one of the axles through one of the wheels. Temporarily position the axle in an axle hole. Pre-drill two fine pilot holes in the mudguard to prevent the wood from splitting when nailed. Line up the mudguard to fit around the wheel without touching it. Glue and nail the mudguard into position using 25 mm bullet head nails. Punch the heads below the surface. Remove the wheel and axle. Repeat the procedure for the remaining wheels. Fill the nail holes with wood filler and sand smooth.

8. Cut out the running board. Glue and nail it to the base of the bus using 12 mm bullet head nails.

9. Paint the body and wheels separately using non-toxic gloss paint.

10. When the paint is dry, pass the axles through the 7 mm holes in the body. Glue the wheels to the axles.

Truck

CUTTING LIST

Pine
220 x 90 x 35 mm — body
300 x 70 x 19 mm — wheels and mudguards
125 x 70 x 12 mm — tray top base
50 x 70 x 12 mm — tray top front

4 mm plywood
55 x 73 mm — running board

6 mm dowelling
Two 78 mm lengths — axles

MATERIALS
15 mm bullet head nails
20 mm bullet head nails
25 mm bullet head nails

EQUIPMENT
25 mm spade bit
7 mm drill bit
50 mm hole saw

INSTRUCTIONS

1. Read through all the instructions. Check the template, assembly chart and photograph before beginning the project. Use a photocopier to enlarge the template to full size. Trace the template diagrams onto the pieces of wood in the cutting list.

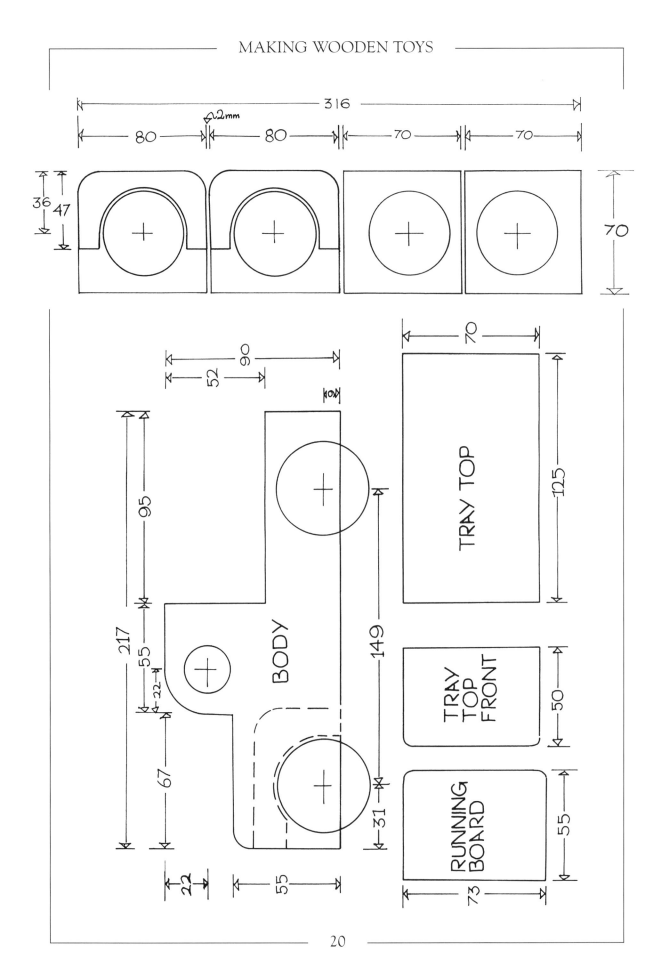

2. Cut out the body.

3. Using a 25 mm spade bit, drill the window hole in the body.

4. Drill two 7 mm axles holes in the body.

5. Using a 50 mm hole saw, cut the four wheels out of the pine block (DO NOT cut the pine block into sections first). The wheels will have a 6 mm hole in the centre for attaching to the axles in step 11.

6. Using a jigsaw or tenon saw, cut the pine block into sections, as marked on the template. Trim the pieces to create the front mudguards. Round off the edges using sandpaper.

7. Positioning the mudguards correctly is important to prevent them from binding on the wheels. Do this by first putting one of the axles through one of the wheels. Temporarily position the axle in an axle hole. Pre-drill two fine pilot holes in a mudguard to prevent the wood from splitting when nailed. Line up the mudguard to fit around the wheel without touching it. Glue and nail the mudguard into position. Use 25 mm bullet head nails and punch the heads below the surface. Remove the wheel and axle. Repeat the procedure for the other front wheel. Fill the holes with wood filler and sand off all sharp edges.

8. Using the assembly chart as a guide, glue and nail the tray top front to the tray top base. Glue and nail this assembly to the body using 20 mm bullet head nails. Punch the heads below the surface and fill the holes. Sand off all sharp edges.

9. Cut out the running board. Glue and nail it to the base of the truck using 15 mm bullet head nails.

10. Paint the body and the wheels separately.

11. When the parts are dry, pass the axles through the 7 mm holes in the body. Glue the wheels to the axles.

Dump Truck

CUTTING LIST

Pine
220 x 90 x 35 mm — body
300 x 70 x 19 mm — wheels and mudguards
125 x 70 x 12 mm — base of tray
50 x 70 x 12 mm — front of tray
125 x 42 x 12 mm — sides of tray

4 mm plywood
55 x 75 mm — running board

6 mm dowelling
Two lengths to 78 mm — axles

MATERIALS
15 mm bullet head nails
20 mm bullet head nails
25 mm bullet head nails

EQUIPMENT
7 mm drill bit
50 mm hole saw
25 mm spade bit

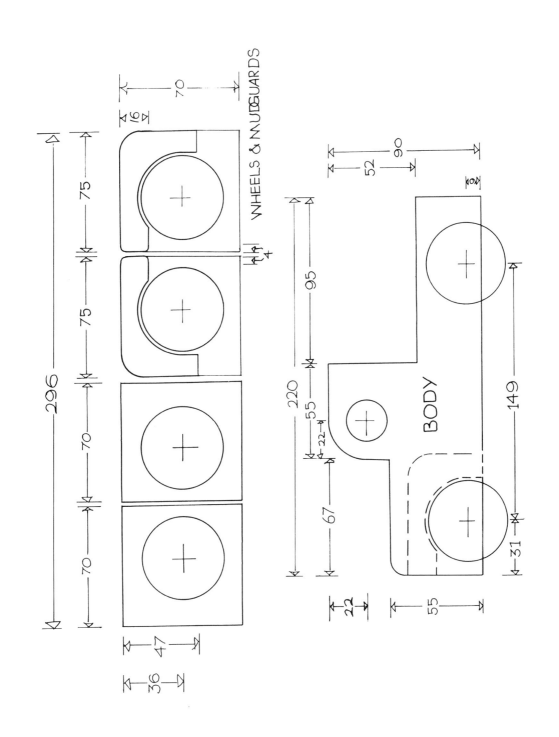

WHEELS & MUDGUARDS

BODY

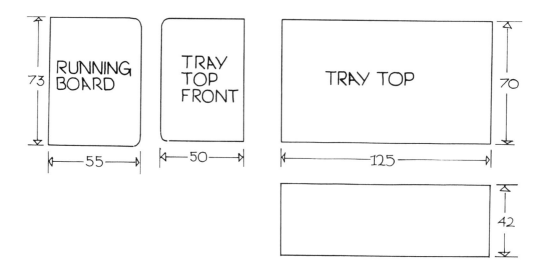

INSTRUCTIONS

1. Read through all the instructions. Check the template and assembly chart and photograph before beginning the project. Use a photocopier to enlarge the template to full size. Trace the template diagrams onto the pieces of wood listed in the cutting list.

2. Cut out the body.

3. Using a 25 mm spade bit, drill one hole in the body in the position marked on the template for the window.

4. Drill two 7 mm axle holes in the positions marked on the template.

5. Using a 50 mm hole saw, cut the four wheels out of the pine block (DO NOT cut the pine block into sections first). The wheels will have a 6 mm hole in the centre for attaching to the axles in step 12.

6. Using a jigsaw or tenon saw, cut the pine block into sections, as marked on the template. Trim the pieces to create the mudguards. Round off the edges using sandpaper.

7. Positioning the mudguards correctly is important to prevent the wheels rubbing on them. Do this by first putting one of the axles through one of the wheels. Temporarily

position the axle in the front axle hole. Pre-drill two, fine pilot holes in the mudguard to prevent the wood from splitting when nailed. Line up the mudguard to fit around the wheel without touching it. Glue and nail the mudguard into position. Use 25 mm bullet head nails and punch the heads below the surface. Remove the wheel and axle. Repeat the procedure for the other front wheel. Fill the holes with wood filler and sand off all sharp edges.

8. Using 20 mm bullet head nails, glue and nail the tray front to the tray base. Then glue and nail the tray sides to the front and base. Glue and nail this assembly to the body. Punch the nail heads below the surface and fill the holes.

9. Cut out the running board. Glue and nail it to the base of truck using 15 mm bullet head nails.

10. Sand off all sharp edges of the body.

11. Paint the body and wheels separately.

12. When dry pass the axles through the body. Glue the wheels to the axles.

Semitrailer

CUTTING LIST

Pine

184 x 90 x 35 mm — body and trailer wheel
support block
445 x 70 x 19 mm — wheels and mudguards
195 x 70 x 12 mm — trailer
12 x 70 x 12 mm — trailer front

6 mm dowelling
Three 78 mm lengths — axles

16 mm dowelling
One 30 mm length — coupling pin

MATERIALS
20 mm bullet head nails
25 mm bullet head nails

EQUIPMENT
7 mm drill bit
16 mm drill bit
50 mm hole saw
25 mm spade bit

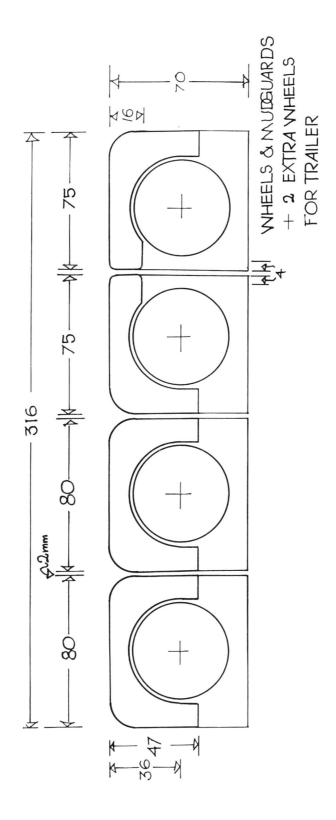

WHEELS & MUDGUARDS
+ 2 EXTRA WHEELS
FOR TRAILER

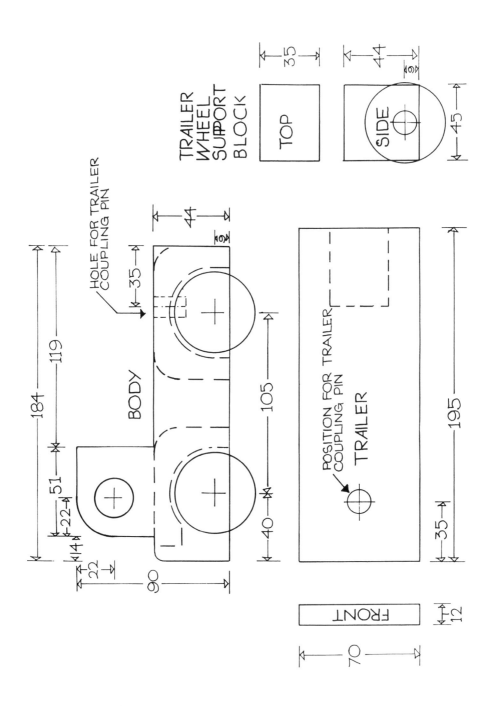

TRAILER
WHEEL
SUPPORT
BLOCK

TOP

SIDE

35

44

45

HOLE FOR TRAILER
COUPLING PIN

BODY

44

35

184

119

51

22

22

14

90

105

40

POSITION FOR TRAILER
COUPLING PIN

TRAILER

195

35

FRONT

12

70

INSTRUCTIONS

1. Read through all the instructions. Check the template and assembly chart and photograph before beginning the project. Use a photocopier to enlarge the template to full size. Trace the template diagrams onto the pieces of wood listed in the cutting list.

2. Cut out the body.

3. From the waste left after cutting out the body, cut out the trailer wheel support block.

4. Using a 25 mm spade bit, the window hole in the body. Drill two 7 mm axle holes through the body. Drill another 7 mm hole through the trailer wheel support block for the trailer axle. Then drill a 16 mm hole in the body for the coupling pin to fit into.

5. Using a 50 mm hole saw, cut the four wheels out of the pine block (DO NOT cut the pine block into sections first). The wheels will have a 6 mm hole in the centre for attaching to the axles in step 11.

6. Using a jigsaw or tenon saw, cut the pine block into sections, as marked on the template. Trim the pieces to create the mudguards. Round off the edges using sandpaper.

7. Positioning the mudguards correctly is important to prevent the wheels rubbing on them. Do this by first putting one of the axles through one of the wheels. Temporarily position the axle in the front axle hole. Pre-drill two fine pilot holes in a front mudguard to prevent the wood from splitting when nailed. Line up the mudguard to fit around the wheel without touching it. Glue and nail the mudguard into position. Use 25 mm bullet head nails and punch the heads below the surface. Remove the wheel and axle. Repeat the procedure for the remaining wheels. Fill the holes with wood filler and sand off all sharp edges.

8. Glue and nail the trailer wheel support block to the underside of the trailer. Glue and nail the front to the top front edge of the trailer. Use 20 mm bullet head nails. Punch the nail heads below the surface and fill the holes.

9. Drill a 16 mm hole (for the coupling pin) in the underside of the trailer, as shown on the template. Glue the coupling pin into the hole. When the glue is dry, trim the pin so that it fits into the corresponding hole in the body.

9. Sand all sharp edges.

10. Paint the body, trailer and wheels separately.

11. When dry, pass the axles though the holes in the body and the trailer wheel support block. Glue on the wheels.

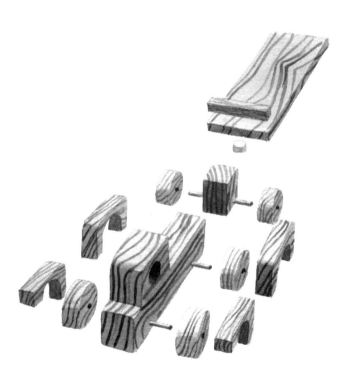

Front-end loader

CUTTING LIST

Pine

130 x 90 x 35 mm — body
300 x 70 x 19 mm — wheels and shovel supports
105 x 45 x 12 mm — shovel back
35 x 45 x 12 mm — shovel sides

4 mm plywood

105 x 50 mm — shovel base

6 mm dowelling

Three 80 mm lengths — wheel axles and shovel axle
One 15 mm length — shovel lift
One 15 mm length — shovel stop

MATERIALS

15 mm bullet head nails
20 mm bullet head nails

EQUIPMENT

7 mm drill bit
50 mm hole saw
25 mm spade bit

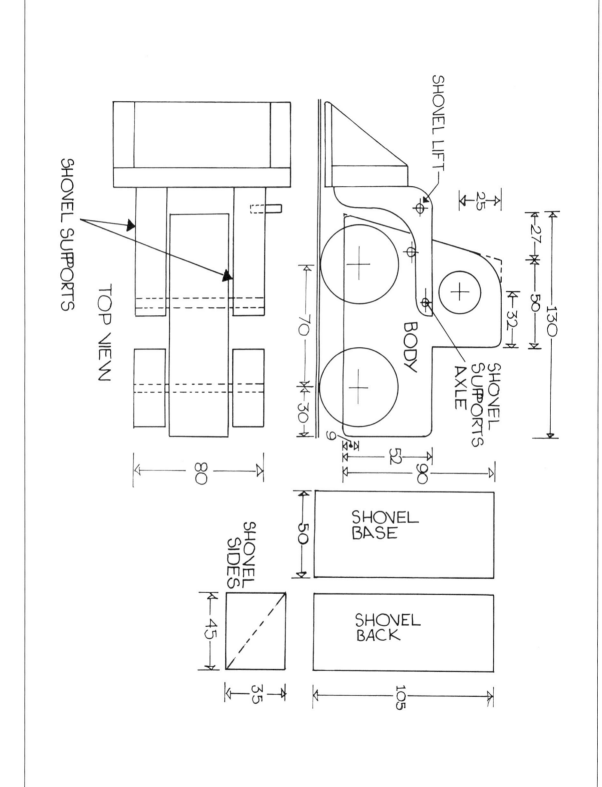

SHOVEL LIFT

SHOVEL SUPORTS AXLE

BODY

SHOVEL SUPPORTS

TOP VIEW

SHOVEL BASE

SHOVEL SIDES

SHOVEL BACK

25

27

50

130

32

70

30

9

52

90

80

50

45

35

105

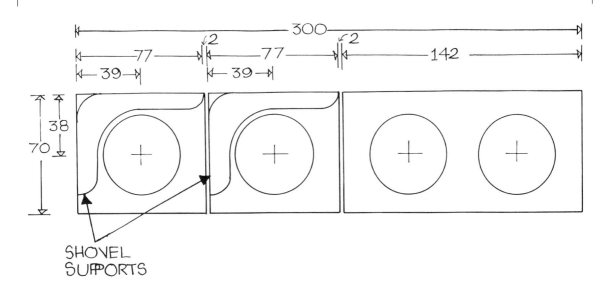

SHOVEL
SUPPORTS

INSTRUCTIONS

1. Read through all the instructions. Check the template and assembly chart and photograph before beginning the project. Use a photocopier to enlarge the template to full size. Trace the template diagrams onto the pieces of wood listed in the cutting list.

2. Cut out the body.

3. Using a 25 mm spade bit, drill the window hole in the body. Next, drill two 7 mm axle holes through the body. Drill a 6 mm hole for shovel axle.

4. Sand off all the edges of the body.

5. Using a 50 mm hole saw, cut out the wheels. (DO NOT cut the block into sections first). Cut the waste that is left into three pieces, as shown in the template. Cut out the shovel supports. Round off the edges with sandpaper.

6. Cut out the back and sides of the shovel. Using the assembly chart as a guide, glue and nail the pieces together using 20 mm bullet head nails.

7. Glue and nail the shovel base to the assembled sides and back. Use 15 mm bullet head nails. Punch the nail heads below the surface and fill the holes. Sand all sharp edges.

8. Drill a 6 mm hole into one shovel side support for the shovel lift. Drill the hole about 10 mm deep. Glue the shovel lift into the hole.

9. Drill a 7 mm axle hole into each shovel support. Tap an axle through one shovel support, through the body then into the other side support. The axle should fit snugly in the body and only the side supports should move. Leave the supports in position.

10. Glue and nail the shovel to the shovel supports using 20 mm bullet head nails. Pre-drill pilot holes in the shovel to prevent the wood from splitting. (Note: if you are building this toy for a child under 3, join the shovel to the shovel supports by drilling 6 mm holes through the shovel and into the supports then joining with dowelling. Fill the holes and sand before painting.)

11. Paint the wheels and assembled body separately.

12. Pass the wheel axles through the axle holes in the body. Glue the wheels to the axles.

Steamroller

CUTTING LIST

Pine
165 x 90 x 35 mm — body
45 x 19 x 70 mm — base
120 x 70 x 35 mm — rollers

18 mm square moulding
Two 165 mm lengths

4 mm plywood or masonite
110 x 30 mm — wheel 'washers'

6 mm dowelling
Two 81 mm lengths — axles

MATERIALS
25 mm bullet head nails
40 mm bullet head nails

EQUIPMENT
25 mm spade bit
25 mm hole saw
50 mm hole saw
7 mm drill bit

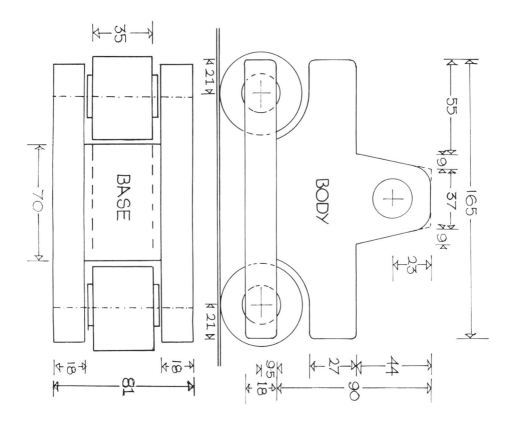

INSTRUCTIONS

1. Read through all the instructions. Check the template and assembly chart and photograph before beginning the project. Use a photocopier to enlarge the template to full size. Trace the template diagrams onto the pieces of wood listed in the cutting list.

2. Cut out the body. Using a 25mm spade bit, drill a hole in the body for the window.

3. Cut out the base. Attach the base to the body using glue and 40 mm bullet head nails.

4. Cut out the two rollers using a 50 mm hole saw. Enlarge the centre holes to 7 mm.

5. Cut out the four 'washers' using a 25 mm hole saw. Enlarge the centre hole to 7 mm. Glue one washer to each side of the rollers making sure the holes line up.

6. Drill four 6 mm axle holes through the square dressed boards, as shown on template.

7. Glue and nail the square dressed boards to the sides of the base. Use 25 mm bullet head nails, punching the nail heads below the surface then filling in the holes. Pre-drill pilot holes to prevent the wood from splitting.

8. Round off all square edges using sandpaper. Paint all but the outside edges of the board.

9. Position the rollers between the square moulding, lining up the axle holes. Tap the axles through the square moulding, rollers and then the square moulding on the other side. Make sure that the axles fit snugly in the square moulding and that the rollers turn freely.

10. Sand the outside edges smooth, then paint.

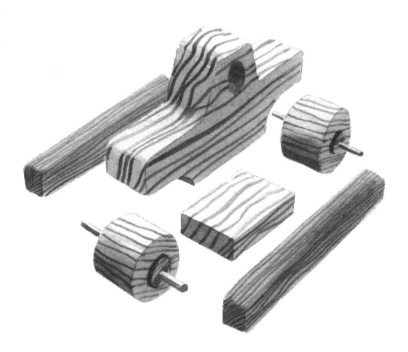

Bulldozer

CUTTING LIST

Pine
160 x 90 x 35 mm — body
450 x 19 x 70 mm — wheels
120 x 15 x 12 mm — blade supports

6 mm dowelling
Two 115 mm lengths — front axles
One 85 mm length — back axle
Two 35 mm length — to attach blade to
side support

4 mm plywood
270 x 30 mm — ten wheel washers

30 mm scotia (cornice)
One 135 mm length — blade

MATERIALS
No nails required

EQUIPMENT
Keyhole saw
25 mm spade bit
50 mm hole saw
25 mm hole saw
7 mm drill bit
6 mm drill bit

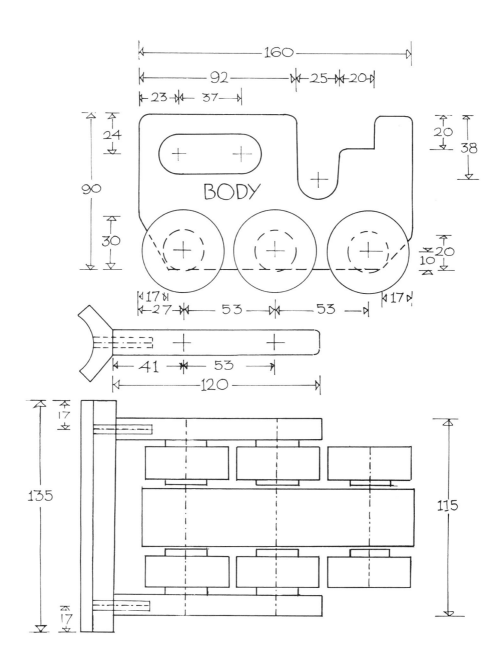

INSTRUCTIONS

1. Read through all the instructions. Check the template and assembly chart and photograph before beginning the project. Use a photocopier to enlarge the template to full size. Trace the template diagrams onto the pieces of wood listed in the cutting list.

2. Mark out from the full sized template onto the body block and mark the centres of the three 25 mm diameter holes and drill using a spade bit, finish cutting out the body with either a keyhole saw or a jigsaw.

3. Drill two 6 mm holes for the front wheel axles and a 7 mm hole for the back wheel axle.

4. Using a 50 mm hole saw, cut out six wheels. In four of the wheels, enlarge the holes to 7 mm. These are the front four wheels. The other two are the back wheels.

5. Cut out the blade supports. Drill two 6 mm axle holes through each support. Drill a 6 mm hole into the other end of each support for joining on the blade.

6. Using a 25 mm hole saw, cut out ten wheel washers. On eight of the washers, enlarge the centre holes to 7 mm. Glue these washers to both sides of the four front wheels making sure the centre holes line up.

7. Glue the remaining two washers to only one side of each of the back wheels, making sure the 6 mm holes line up.

8. Drill two 6 mm holes through the blade, 17 mm from each end. Attach the blade to the blade supports using 6 mm dowelling. Sand off any dowelling protruding through the blade or fill any holes.

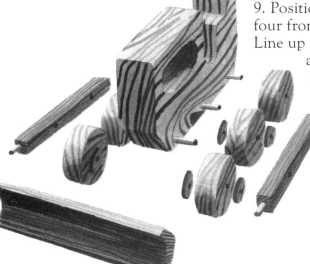

9. Position the blade supports, the four front wheels and the body. Line up the holes and tap the front axles through. The wheels should rotate not the axles.

10. Pass the back axle through the body. Glue on the wheels so that the washers are facing towards the body.

11. Sand and paint.

Plane

CUTTING LIST

Pine

275 x 60 x 35 mm — fuselage
250 x 70 x 12 mm — wings
70 x 70 x 12 mm — rudder
125 x 40 x 12 mm — tail wing
109 x 25 x 12 mm — wheel supports
160 x 42 x 12 mm — wheels

6 mm dowelling

One 30 mm length — to attach tail wing to rudder
Three 25 mm lengths — to attach wheel supports

MATERIALS

Three 25 mm x 8 gauge round head screws
20 mm bullet head nails

EQUIPMENT

Keyhole saw
38 mm hole saw
25 mm spade bit

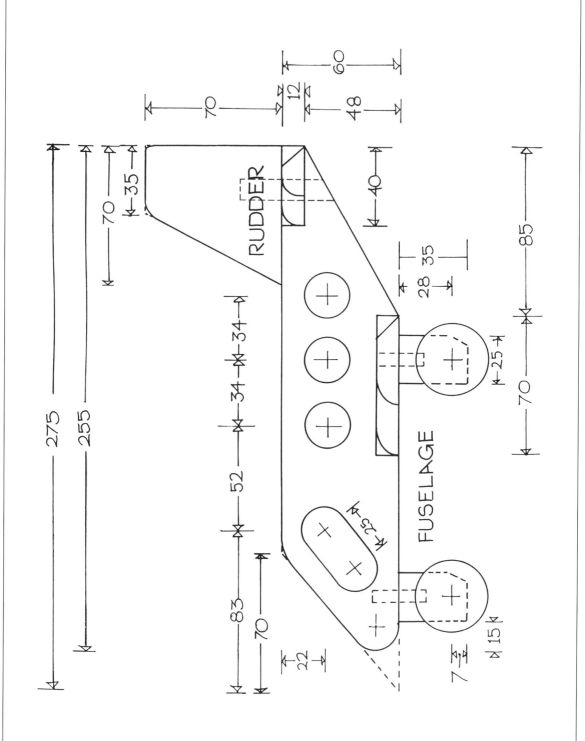

RUDDER

FUSELAGE

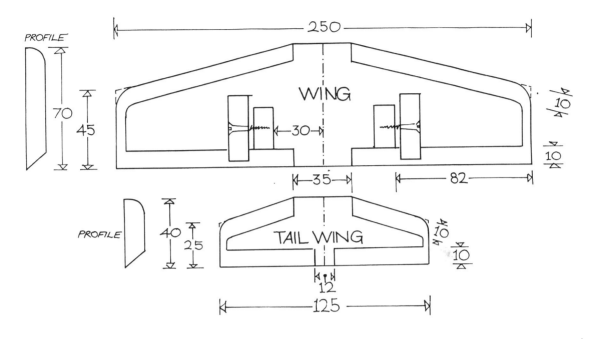

INSTRUCTIONS

1. Read through all the instructions. Check the template and assembly chart and photograph before beginning the project. Use a photocopier to enlarge the template to full size. Trace the template diagrams onto the pieces of wood listed in the cutting list.

2. Cut out the fuselage.

3. Using a 25 mm spade bit, drill five holes for the windows. Cut out the waste between the two front holes using a keyhole drill.

4. Cut out the wings, tail wings and rudder. Using a rasp and sandpaper, shape the front and rear edges as shown on the template.

5. Glue and nail the wings to the bottom of the fuselage. Use 20 mm bullet head nails. Punch the heads below the surface and fill the holes.

6. Attach the tail wings to the rudder using 6 mm dowelling. Do this by first drilling a 6 mm hole through the centre of the tail wing. Line up the rudder on the tail wing and mark the position for the corresponding hole on the base of the rudder. Then, drill a hole about 20 mm deep into the base of the rudder. Tap the piece of

dowelling into place in the rudder and then through the tail wing. Trim or sand off any dowelling that may be protruding through the underside of the tail wing. (NOTE: I have used dowelling here to prevent the possibility of injury from a protruding nail if the rudder is broken off during play.)

7. Glue and nail the tail assembly to the fuselage. Use a 20 mm bullet head nail each side of rudder. Punch the heads below the surface and fill the holes.

8. Sand off any sharp edges.

9. Cut the wheel supports piece of pine into three sections. Each piece should be roughly 35 mm long. Shape off one corner of each piece as shown in the template. In the centre of the opposite end, drill a 6 mm diameter hole to about 15 mm deep. Drill roughly corresponding 6 mm diameter holes under the nose of the plane and under the wings to a depth of about 12 mm. Tap the dowelling into these holes then tap on the wheel supports.

10. Use a 38 mm hole saw to cut the three wheels. Attach them to the supports with the round head screws.

11. Paint.

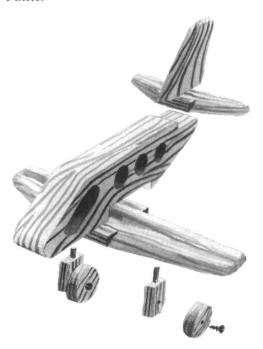

Four-Wheel Drive

CUTTING LIST

Pine

600 x 120 x 12 mm — side panels
125 x 70 x 45 mm — front block
100 x 70 x 45 mm — rear block
250 x 70 x 12 mm — Four 50 mm diameter wheels

4 mm plywood

270 x 70 mm — floor
95 x 94 mm — roof
30 x 70 mm — seat back
25 mm diameter disc — steering wheel

Moulding

46 mm length of 12 mm half-round —
floor console
Two 94 mm lengths of 19 x 7 mm —
front & back bumper bar
Two 27 mm lengths of 19 x 7 mm —
front sides of bumper bar
Two 25 mm lengths of 19 x 7 mm —
back sides of bumper bar

4 mm dowelling

Two lengths to 100 mm — axles
One length to 20 mm — steering wheel shaft
One length to 25 mm — gear shift

MATERIALS
Four 6 mm screw eyes
12 mm flat head nails

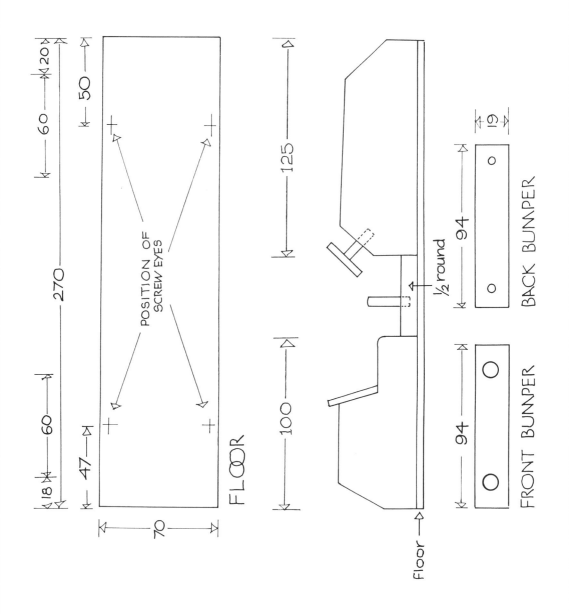

20 mm flat head nails
25 mm flat head nails
25 mm bullet head nails

EQUIPMENT
6 mm drill bit
8 mm drill bit
50 mm hole saw
25 mm spade bit

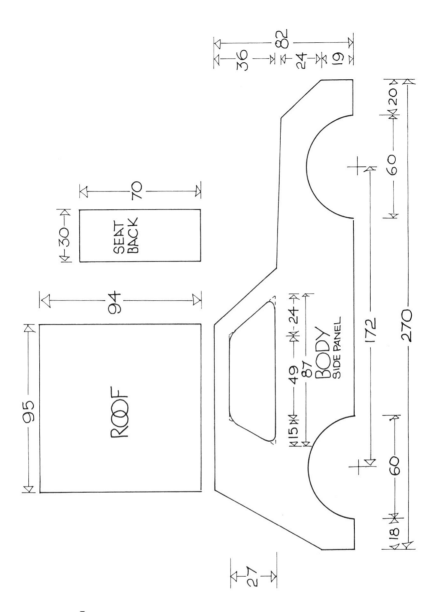

INSTRUCTIONS

1. Read through all the instructions. Check the template and assembly chart and photograph before beginning the project. Use a photocopier to enlarge the template to full size. Trace the template diagrams onto the pieces of wood listed in the cutting list.

2. Cut out the two side panels.

3. Cut out the front and rear blocks. Glue and nail these blocks to the floor as shown in diagram A. Use 25 mm flat head nails.

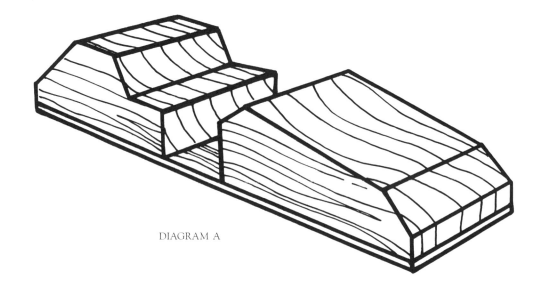

DIAGRAM A

4. Using a 6 mm drill, make a hole 10 mm deep in the dashboard of the front block for the steering wheel column. Glue in the 20 mm length of dowelling. On to this glue the 25 mm diameter plywood disc.

5. Glue the half-round dowelling to the centre of the floor between the front and rear blocks. Drill a 6 mm hole in the top of the half-round dowelling, in the position shown in the template. Glue in the gear shift.

6. Using 20 mm flat head nails, glue and nail the side panels to the sides of the front and rear blocks. Making sure that the panels line up with the ends of the blocks.

7. Using 12 mm flat head nails, glue and nail the roof to the top of the side panels. Sand the front and back of the roof to the same angle as the side panels.

8. Drill two 8 mm holes in the front bumper bar for the headlights and two 6 mm holes in the rear bumper for the tail lights. Using 25 mm bullet head nails, glue and nail the bumper bars to the front and rear of the assembled body. Then, glue and nail the sides of the bumper bars. Use a rasp and sandpaper to round off the bumper corners.

Above: Cradle

Right: Car

Below: Bus

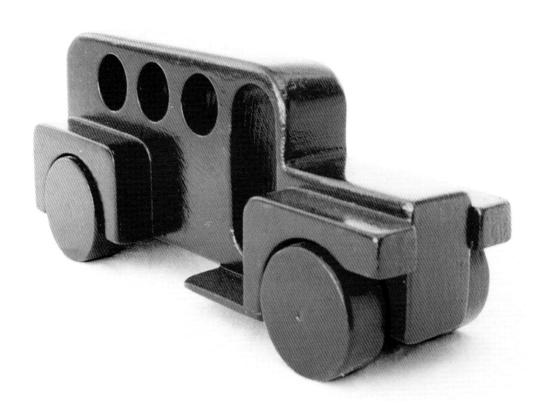

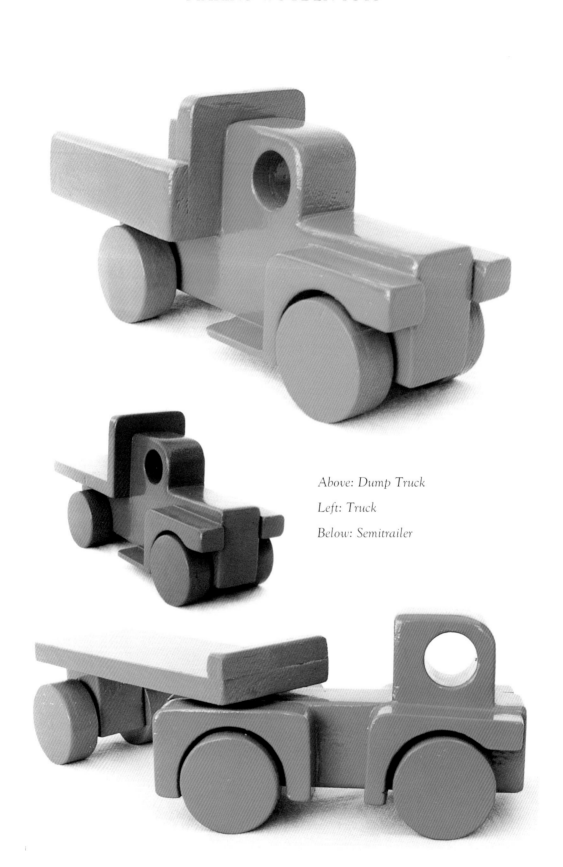

Above: Dump Truck

Left: Truck

Below: Semitrailer

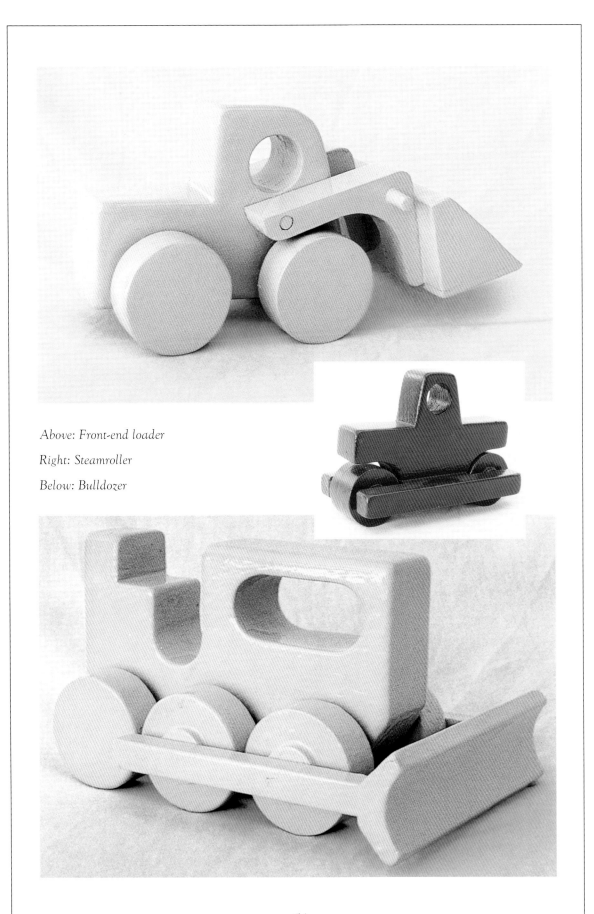

Above: Front-end loader

Right: Steamroller

Below: Bulldozer

Above:
Four-wheel drive

Centre:
Plane

Below:
Tip truck

Above: Jeep

Right: Pram

Left: Grader

Right: Jet

Below: Train, flat car and box car

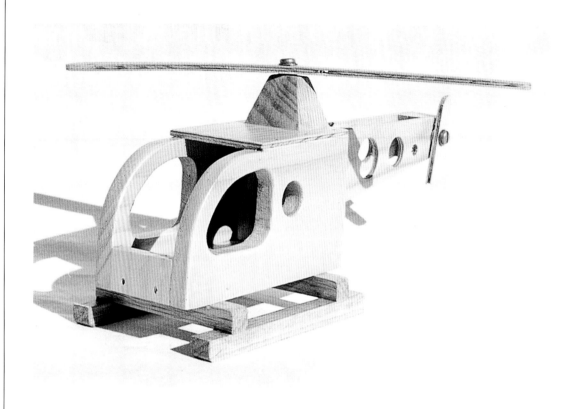

Above: Helicopter

Right: Sewing machine

9. Cut out the four wheels, as follows. Using a 50 mm hole saw, cut about half way through. Then, with a 25 mm spade bit, line up the centre hole and drill down about 3 mm. Finish cutting the wheels out with the hole saw.

10. The axles are attached to the floor of the car by 6 mm screw eyes in the position shown on the template diagram. Pass the dowelling axles through the screw eyes and glue on the wheels.

11. Paint.

Tip Truck

CUTTING LIST

Pine

470 x 120 x 12 mm — cab side panels and mud-guards
94 x 67 x 12 mm — grill
88 x 70 x 12 mm — back of cab
140 x 25 x 12 mm — bumper bar
80 x 70 x 45 mm — front (engine)
290 x 70 x 19 mm — base
90 x 120 x 12 mm — front of tip truck
190 x 120 x 12 mm — floor of truck
37 x 120 x 12 mm — back of truck
160 x 70 x 19 mm — underside of tip truck floor
400 x 70 x 19 mm — wheels

4 mm plywood

94 x 50 mm — roof of cab
Two 200 x 50 mm lengths — sides of truck

Moulding

Two 70 mm lengths of 12 mm square moulding
Two 45 mm lengths of 19 mm half-round moulding

4 mm dowelling

One 155 mm length — back axle
One 142 mm length — front axle

MATERIALS

Four 6 mm screw eyes
Two 6 mm washers
Two 6 gauge x 10 mm self tapping screws

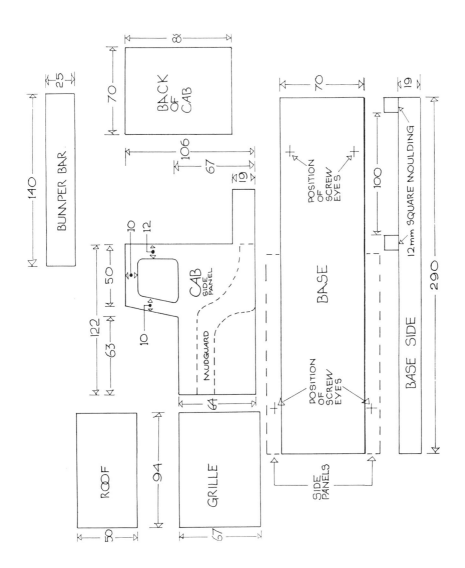

Hinge to 70 mm long
12 mm bullet head nails
20 mm bullet head nails
25 mm bullet heads nails

EQUIPMENT
4 mm drill bit
50 mm hole saw
6 mm drill bit
25 mm spade bit

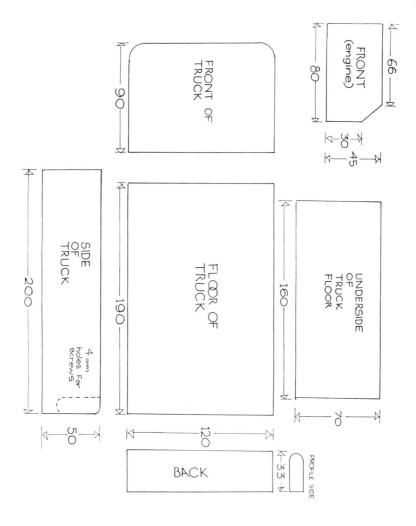

INSTRUCTIONS

1. Read through all the instructions. Check the template and assembly chart and photograph before beginning the project. Use a photocopier to enlarge the template to full size. Trace the template diagrams onto the pieces of wood listed in the cutting list.

2. Using a jig saw, cut out the side panels. From the waste, cut out the mudguards. Make the windows in the side panels by first drilling four 6 mm holes for the corners, then cutting out the waste using a jigsaw or key hole saw.

3. Cut the front (engine). Using the template as a guide, trim off one edge to make the dashboard. Glue and nail it flush to the end of the base using 25 mm bullet head nails. Glue and nail the side panels to this assembly using 20 mm bullet head nails.

4. Next, glue and nail the mudguards to the side panels in the position shown as a broken line in the template. Follow the procedure described in earlier projects for making sure the mudguards do not rub on the wheels. Use 20 mm bullet head nails, punch the heads below the surface and fill.

5. Glue and nail the back and roof of the cab in position using 12 mm bullet heads. Next, glue and nail on the grill and bumper bar using 20 mm bullet heads. Punch heads below the surface and fill.

6. Glue the lengths of half-round moulding onto the side panels behind the mudguards (see photograph). Using 20 mm bullet head nails,

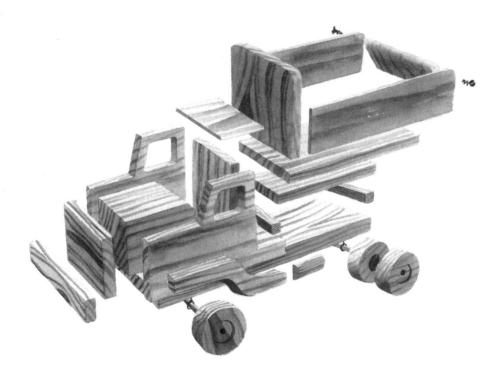

glue and nail the lengths of 12 mm square moulding to the top of the base in the positions marked on the template.

7.   Glue and nail the front of the truck to the end of the tip truck floor using 25 mm bullet head nails. Punch heads below the surface and fill.

8.   Using 25 mm bullet head nails, glue and nail the underside of the tip truck to the bottom of the floor. Make sure the underside is centred and flush with the front of the floor.

9.   Drill two 4 mm holes in the truck sides in position shown in the template. The sides of the truck are glued and nailed to the sides of the floor and front using 12 mm bullet head nails. Punch the heads below the surface and fill.

10.   Place the truck back into position and mark the spots that correspond to the 4 mm holes in the sides. Remove the back and drill pilot holes for screws. Replace the back and pass the self tapping screws through the sides and screw them into the back of the tip truck. To make sure the back swings freely you may need to sand off the sides of the back a little.

11.   Screw the hinge under the back end of the truck floor. Screw the other half of the hinge to the rear end of the 12 mm square moulding on the base of the truck.

12.   Cut two wheels using a 50 mm hole saw. Cut the remaining four wheels by cutting half way through with a 50 mm hole saw. Then, with a 25 mm spade bit, line up the centre hole and drill down about 3 mm. Finish cutting the wheels out with the hole saw. These are the two outside wheels for the back and the two wheels for the front.

13.   The axles are held in position by 6 mm screw eyes in position shown on the template diagram.

14.   Pass the axles through the screw eyes, 155 mm length to back. Glue on single wheels at the front, double wheels at the back separated by the 6 mm washers.

15.   Paint.

Jeep

CUTTING LIST

Pine

500 x 70 x 12 mm — side panels
55 x 70 x 12 mm — back
64 x 70 x 12 mm — grill
194 x 70 x 19 mm — floor
25 x 70 x 19 mm — seat
62 x 70 x 19 mm — inside back
75 x 70 x 45 mm — engine
340 x 70 x 19 mm — wheels

12 mm square moulding

Two lengths to 94 mm — bumper bars

6 mm dowelling

Two lengths to 105 mm long — axles
One length to 20 mm long — tow bar
One length to 25 mm long — steering wheel shaft

4 mm plywood

Two pieces laminated 80 x 70 mm — windscreen
Two pieces 20 x 49 mm — seat backs
One piece 25 x 55 mm — tow bar
One 19 mm diameter disc — steering wheel

MATERIALS

Four 6 mm screw eyes
12 mm bullet head nails
20 mm bullet head nails
25 mm bullet head nails
30 mm bullet head nails

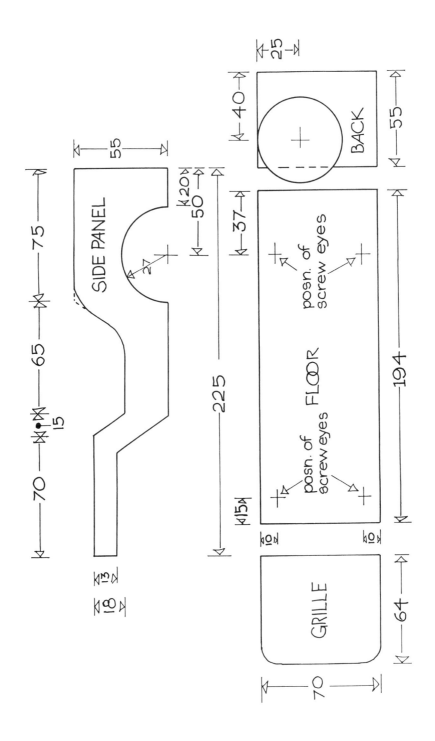

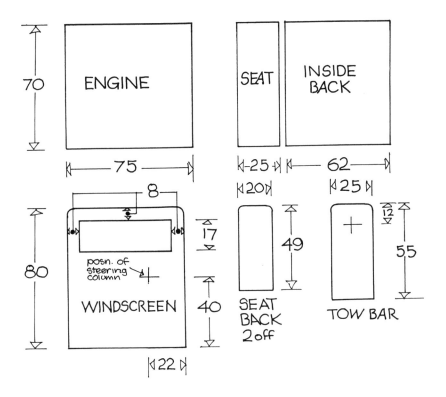

40 mm bullet head nails
15 mm bullet head nails
20 mm 8 gauge round head screw

EQUIPMENT
8 mm drill bit
6 mm drill bit

INSTRUCTIONS

1. Read through all the instructions. Check the
    template and assembly chart and photograph
    before beginning the project. Use a
    photocopier to enlarge the template to full size.
    Trace the template diagrams onto the pieces of
    wood listed in the cutting list.

2. Cut out side panels.

Ply seat backs

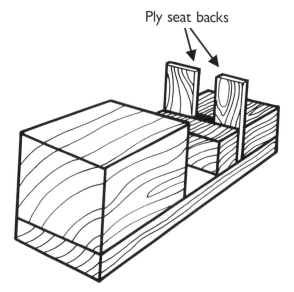

DIAGRAM E

3. Cut out the floor. Next, glue and nail the engine floor, flush with one end, using 40 mm bullet head nails.

4. Glue together (laminate) two pieces of plywood for the windscreen. When dry, cut out the window by drilling four holes at the corners then cutting out the waste in between. Glue and nail it to the back of the engine using 20 mm bullet head nails.

5. Drill a 6 mm hole 10 mm deep at about a 30 degree angle just below the windscreen, as shown in the template. Glue the steering wheel shaft into the hole.

6. Cut out the seats. Then, cut two seat backs, as shown in the template. Using 12 mm bullet head nails, glue and nail them to the seat, as shown in diagram E.

7. Using 25 mm bullet head nails, glue and nail the inside back to the floor, making sure it lines up with the end of the base.

8. Glue and nail the seat assembly to the base using 25 mm bullet head nails, as shown in the diagram E.

9. Using 30 mm bullet head nails, glue and nail the grill to the front of the engine.

10. Using 30 mm bullet head nails, glue and nail the back to the base.

11. Glue and nail the side panels to the body assembly using 25 mm bullet head nails.

12. Glue and nail the bumper bars to the front and rear of the body, using 15 mm bullet head nails.

13. Using a 50mm hole saw, cut out five wheels. One wheel is the spare and is screwed to the back of the jeep in the position shown in the template.

14. With a 19 mm hole saw, cut out the steering wheel and glue it onto the steering wheel shaft.

15. Cut the tow bar to the size shown in the template diagram. Drill a 6 mm hole in the tow bar and glue in the dowelling. Glue and nail this assembly to the underside of the back with about 25 mm protruding and the dowelling facing up.

16. Position the four screw eyes in the bottom of the jeep. Pass the axles through the screw eyes. Glue the wheels to the axles.

17. Paint.

Pram

CUTTING LIST

Pine

115 x 70 x 12 mm — floor of pram
69 x 70 x 12 mm — front and back of pram
60 x 70 x 12 mm — hood front
69 x 70 x 12 mm — hood top
270 x 70 x 12 mm — wheels

4 mm plywood

90 x 195 mm — pram sides
100 x 64 mm — hood sides

12 mm square moulding

Two 137 mm lengths — handle shafts

6 mm dowelling

Two 107 mm lengths — axles
One 78 mm length — handle

MATERIALS
Hinge — any size to fit up to 70 mm
12 mm bullet head nails
20 mm bullet head nails

EQUIPMENT
8 mm drill bit
6 mm drill bit
50 mm hole saw
25 mm spade bit

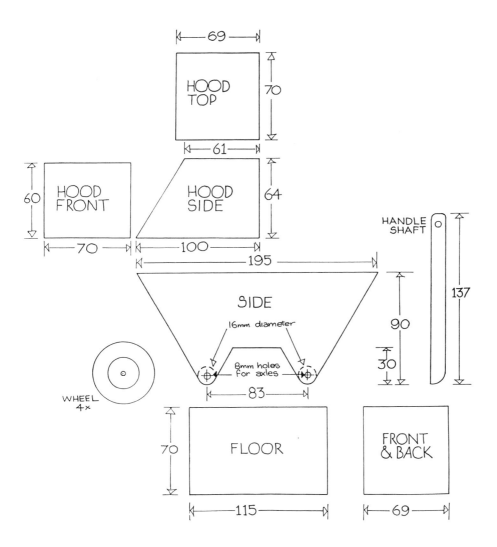

INSTRUCTIONS

1. Read through all the instructions. Check the template and assembly chart and photograph before beginning the project. Use a photocopier to enlarge the template to full size. Trace the template diagrams onto the pieces of wood listed in the cutting list.

2. Cut out the pram sides and the hood sides.

3. Drill two 8 mm axle holes in each of the pram sides.

4. Glue and nail the front and back between the side panels using 12 mm bullet head nails. Using a rasp and sandpaper, bevel the ends of the pram floor to fit between the front and back of the pram. Glue and nail the pram floor in place using 20 mm bullet head nails. Sand off any rough edges.

5. Make up the hood by beveling one end of the hood top to line up with the angle of the hood sides. Glue and nail together the sides to the top using 12 mm bullet head nails.

6. Cut the front of the hood. Bevel the ends to fit flush with the hood top and the top of the pram front. Glue and nail the hood front between the sides using 12 mm bullet head nails. Sand off any rough edges.

7. Round off the edges of the handle shafts, as shown on the template. Drill 6 mm holes at one end of each shaft, making the centres of the holes 10 mm from the end of the shaft.

8. Glue the handle into the holes at the ends of the shafts. Then glue and nail the shafts to the pram. Make sure the edges of the shafts are flush with the pram sides.

9. Attach the hood assembly to the pram with the hinge. You will probably need to pre-drill pilot holes for the nails to stop the wood from splitting.

10. To make a wheel with a hub, cut halfway through the block with a 50 mm hole saw. Then, with a 25 mm spade bit, line up the centre hole and drill down about 3 mm. Finish cutting the wheel out with the hole saw. Repeat to make four wheels.

11. Pass the axles through the holes in the side panels and glue the wheels to the axles.

12. Paint. You may wish to decorate the pram using stencils which are available from most craft shops.

Grader

CUTTING LIST

Pine
210 x 90 x 35 mm — body, front wheel block
420 x 70 x 19 mm — wheels

6 mm dowelling
Three lengths to 85 mm long — axles
One length to 30 mm — to attach grader blade
support to body
One length to 22 mm long — to attach grader blade
to support
Two lengths to 50 mm — to attach front wheel
support to body

4 mm plywood
Scrap piece to cut six 25 mm diameter 'washers'

30 mm scotia (cornice)
One 130 mm length — blade

22 mm dowelling
One 35 mm length — blade support

MATERIALS
40 mm bullet head nails

EQUIPMENT
38 mm hole saw
25 mm hole saw

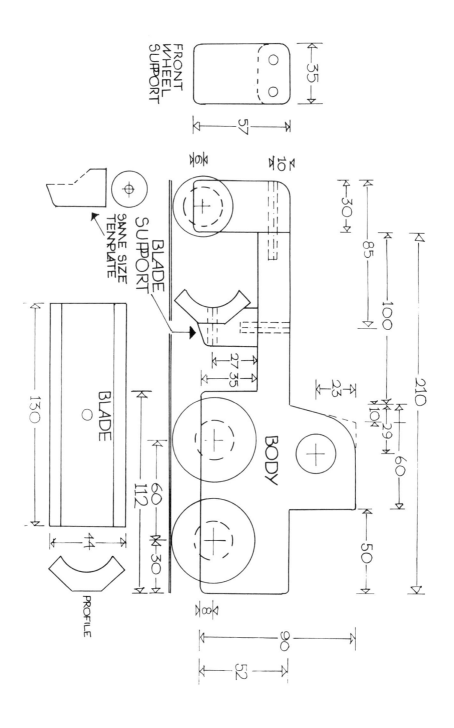

FRONT
WHEEL
SUPPORT

35

57

BLADE
SUPPORT

SAME SIZE
TEMPLATE

BLADE

PROFILE

BODY

10

30

85

100

210

9

23

104

29

60

50

27
35

130

112

60
30

44

8

90

52

INSTRUCTIONS

1. Read through all the instructions. Check the template and assembly chart and photograph before beginning the project. Use a photocopier to enlarge the template to full size. Trace the template diagrams onto the pieces of wood listed in the cutting list.

2. Cut out the body.

3. From the waste left after cutting out the body, cut a 57 mm piece for the front wheel support.

4. Use a 25 mm spade bit to drill a hole for the window.

5. Next, attach the front wheels support to the body. Drill two 6 mm holes through the front wheel support, in the positions marked on template. Line up the front wheel support with the front end of body. Mark the corresponding position on the body. Remove the front wheel support and drill into the body to about 50 mm. Put some glue in the holes and tap in the dowelling, then tap the wheel support onto the dowelling. Sand or rasp off the sides to make a neat join, if necessary.

6. Drill two 7 mm axle holes through the body and one 7 mm axle hole through the front wheel support.

7. Round off all edges on the body using sand paper.

8. To make the blade support, cut out the 22 mm dowelling using the template as a guide. Drill a corresponding 6 mm hole through the blade support and into the back of the blade. Attach the blade to the blade support using 6 mm dowelling. Trim off any dowelling that is protruding.

9. Drill a hole in the centre of the top of the blade support. Place a little glue in the hole and tap the 30 mm length of dowelling into the hole. Drill a 6 mm hole through the grader body then tap the blade support dowelling into the hole. Trim off any dowelling that is protruding from the top of the grader body, or fill the hole if necessary.

10. With a 50 mm hole saw, cut out the four rear wheels. Then, with a 38 mm hole saw, cut out the two front wheels.

11. Using a 25 mm hole saw, cut the six washers from the scrap of plywood. The washers go between the wheels and the body.

12. Glue the washers to the wheels. Make sure the centre holes line up exactly.

13. Pass the axles through the body. Glue on the wheels making sure that the washers face towards the body.

14. Paint.

Jet

CUTTING LIST

Pine

610 x 43 x 12 mm — fuselage side panels
550 x 90 x 12 mm — wing and tail
200 x 55 x 12 mm — tail wing
30 x 20 x 12 mm — engine pylons
145 x 43 x 19 mm — cockpit front middle section
90 x 18 x 19 mm — tail middle section
70 x 43 x 19 mm — engine fronts
100 x 43 x 12 mm — wheels

4 mm plywood

250 x 43 mm — fuselage tops
200 x 40 mm — undercarriage legs

20 mm round moulding

Two 35 mm lengths — engine rear

12 mm square moulding

Three 35 mm lengths — undercarriage leg supports

6 mm dowelling

Three 20 mm lengths — undercarriage axles

4 mm dowelling

Two 20 mm lengths — to fix engine and engine
supports to wing

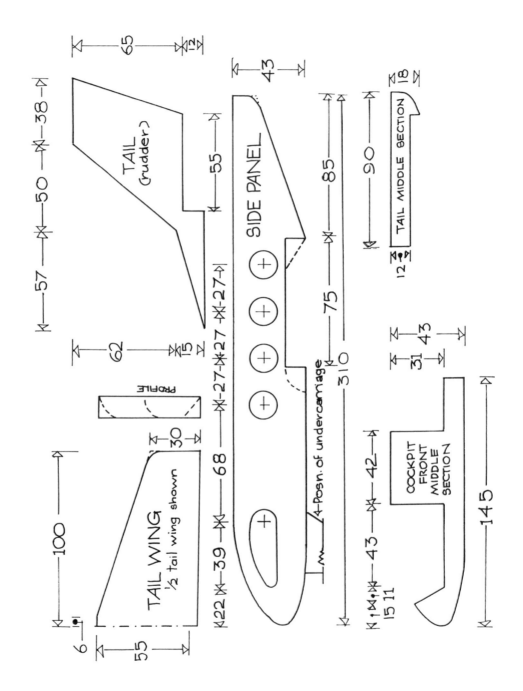

TAIL (rudder)

65 — 12

38 — 50 — 57

55

SIDE PANEL

43

85 — 75 — 310

90

TAIL MIDDLE SECTION

18 — 12

PROFILE

62 — 15

27 — 27 — 27

68 — 39 — 22

Posn. of undercarriage

31 — 43

COCKPIT FRONT MIDDLE SECTION

43 — 42

15 11

145

TAIL WING
½ tail wing shown

30 — 100 — 6

55

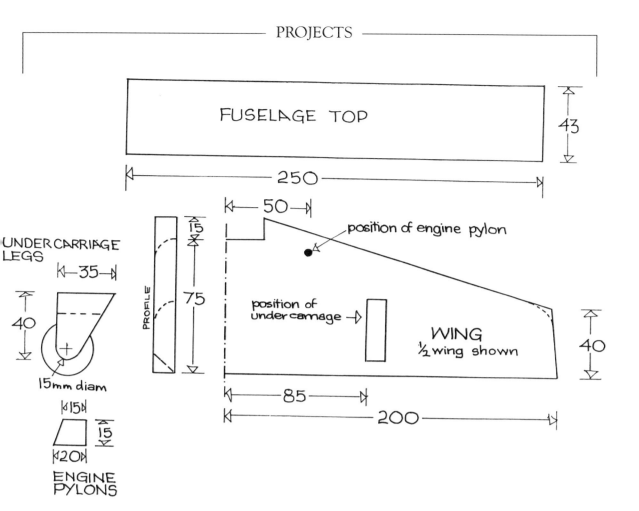

FUSELAGE TOP

43

250

UNDERCARRIAGE LEGS

35

40

15mm diam

PROFILE

15

75

50

position of engine pylon

position of undercarriage →

WING
½ wing shown

40

85

200

15

15

20

ENGINE PYLONS

MATERIALS
Three 6 gauge 20 mm screws
12 mm bullet head nails
20 mm bullet head nails
25 mm flat head nails

EQUIPMENT
19 mm hole saw
8 mm drill bit

INSTRUCTIONS

1. Read through all the instructions. Check the template and assembly chart and photograph before beginning the project. Use a photocopier to enlarge the template to full size. Trace the template diagrams onto the pieces of wood listed in the cutting list.

2. Cut out the side panels of the fuselage. Use a 19 mm hole saw to cut out the portholes. The cockpit window is cut using a 19 mm hole saw at the rear and an 8 mm drill at the front. Cut out the waste with a jigsaw.

3. Next, cut out the wing, tail (rudder), and tail wing. Shape the wing and tail wing to a quarter round on the leading edge. Bevel the trailing edge. See template diagram.

4. Cut out the cockpit front section and the tail middle section. Shape to the template. Glue and nail them between the fuselage sides using 25 mm bullet head nails. Punch the heads below the surface and fill the holes.

5. Glue and nail the wing to the slot in the assembled fuselage using 25 mm flat head nails.

6. Glue and nail the tail wing to the tail. Use 20 mm bullet head nails and nail from underneath into the base of the tail.

7. Glue and nail the fuselage top to the side panels using 12 mm bullet head nails. Punch the heads below the surface and fill the holes.

8. Cut out six undercarriage legs. Drill 6 mm holes in the positions marked on the template.

9. Trim the undercarriage leg supports so that one end is the same angle as the rear of the undercarriage legs. Use 20 mm 6 gauge screws to attach the undercarriage supports to the wing and fuselage, in the positions shown on the template.

10. Using a 32 mm hole saw, cut out three wheels. Enlarge the centre hole to 7 mm diameter.

11. Make up the undercarriage legs by passing the axles through one undercarriage leg, then a wheel, then another leg. Make sure the wheel turns and dowelling sits tightly in the undercarriage legs. Position these assemblies on the undercarriage leg supports. Glue and nail them using 12 mm bullet head nails.

12. The jet engines are constructed by cutting two 32 mm discs using a hole saw. Glue and nail these discs to the engine rears.

13. Cut out the two engine pylons using the template as a guide to shape. Give the wider end a concave shape so that it fits the shape of the engine rear. Drill a 4 mm hole through the engine rear, the pylon and the wing. Assemble these parts using glue and 4 mm dowelling.

14. Before attaching the tail assembly to the fuselage, check that the plane is evenly balanced. To do this, position the tail assembly about 10 mm from the end of fuselage. If the plane overbalances, move the tail assembly further forward. If not, then glue and nail the tail assembly into position.

15. Paint.

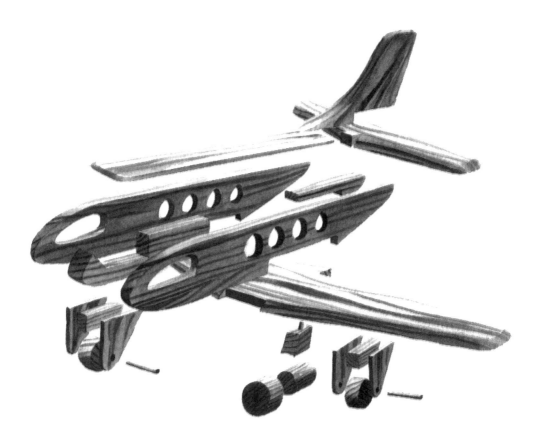

Train
Tank engine

CUTTING LIST

Pine

255 x 120 x 12 mm — front and rear side panels

75 x 70 x 12 mm — front inside cab panel

105 x 77 x 12 mm — cab top

110 x 70 x 45 mm — front block

30 x 70 x 45 mm — rear block

110 x 50 x 19 mm — boiler top

225 x 42 x 12 mm — undercarriage top

220 x 42 x 12 mm — undercarriage bottom

115 x 20 x 12 mm — cow catcher

480 x 70 x 19 mm — wheels

4 mm plywood

200 x 94 mm — floor

6 mm dowelling

Three 85 mm length — axles

One 30 mm length — coupling

16 mm dowelling

One 50 mm length — funnel

One 30 mm length — rear safety valve

MATERIALS

Three 6 gauge 35 mm countersunk screws

Six 6 mm screw eyes

12 mm bullet head nails

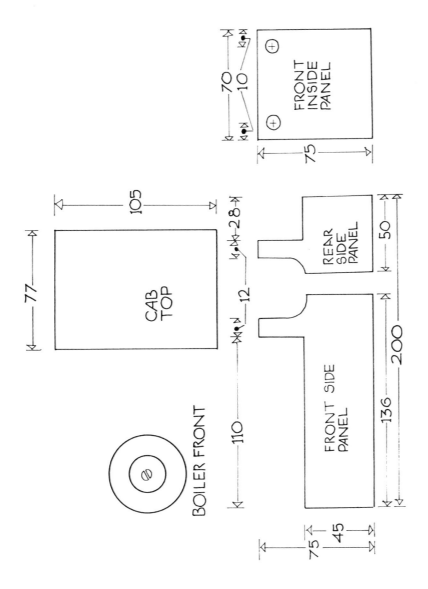

FRONT
INSIDE
PANEL

70
10

75

CAB
TOP

105

77

28

12

REAR
SIDE
PANEL

50

200

136

FRONT SIDE
PANEL

110

BOILER FRONT

75

45

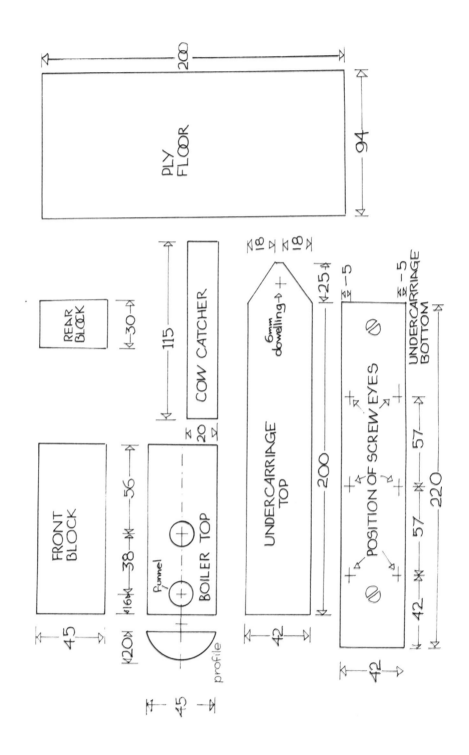

20 mm bullet head nails
30 mm bullet head nails

EQUIPMENT
6 mm drill bit
9 mm drill bit
16 mm spade bit
50 mm hole saw
25 mm spade bit

INSTRUCTIONS

1. Read through all the instructions. Check the template and assembly chart and photograph before beginning the project. Use a photocopier to enlarge the template to full size. Trace the template diagrams onto the pieces of wood listed in the cutting list.

2. Cut out the front and rear side panels.

3. Cut out the front and rear blocks. Glue and nail the side panels to the blocks using 20 mm bullet head nails. Glue and nail the floor to the assembled body using 12 mm bullet head nails. (See diagram C)

5. Drill two 9 mm holes in the front inside cab panel, in the positions shown on the template. Glue and nail the panel to the front block, as shown in the assembly chart. Use 20 mm bullet head nails.

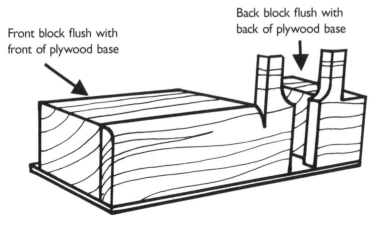

Front block flush with front of plywood base

Back block flush with back of plywood base

DIAGRAM C

This face to be flush with
front of assembled engine

DIAGRAM D

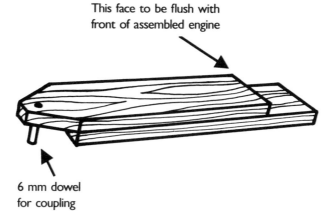

6 mm dowel
for coupling

6. Cut out the boiler top. Round off the top to match the curve of a 50 mm diameter wheel. Drill two 16 mm holes in the top of the boiler to 10 mm deep in position shown in the template diagram. Glue and nail the boiler top of the front block using 30 mm bullet head nails. Sand off rough edges.

7. To make the boiler front, cut one of the wheels, as follows. Using the 50 mm hole saw cut half way through the piece of pine. Then, with the 25 mm spade bit, line up the centre holes and drill to about 4 mm deep. Finish cutting the wheel out with the 50 mm hole saw. Screw the boiler front onto the front block using a countersunk screw. The curve of the boiler front should line up with the curve of the boiler top.

8. Cut the roof of the driver's cab. Curve the edges, as shown on the template. Glue and nail the roof to the top of the cabin using 20 mm bullet head nails.

9. Glue the funnel and the rear safety valve into the boiler top.

10. Cut out the undercarriage top and the undercarriage bottom. Using the template as a guide, taper the end of the undercarriage top. Drill a 6 mm hole in the undercarriage top, as shown on the template.

11. To assemble the undercarriage, glue and nail the undercarriage top and the undercarriage bottom together using 20 mm bullet head nails,

as shown in diagram D. Glue the 6 mm dowelling coupling into the hole in the undercarriage top, so that it extends downwards. See diagram D.

12. Using two of the countersunk screws, attach the undercarriage assembly to the base of the assembled engine. The tapered end of the undercarriage should be facing to the rear and the coupling extending downwards. The front edge of the undercarriage top should line up flush with the front of the front block.

13. Nail and glue the cowcatcher to the front of the bottom undercarriage assembly. Sand off any rough edges on the assembled edges.

14. Using the 50 mm hole saw, cut out the remaining six wheels. DO NOT drill hubs on these wheels.

15. Paint the wheels and the tank engine separately.

16. Screw the six 6 mm screw eyes into the undercarriage, as shown in the template. Pass the axles through the screw eyes. Glue the wheels onto the axles.

Train
Flat car

CUTTING LIST

Pine
180 x 85 x 12 mm — base
30 x 85 x 12 mm — ends
Two 50 x 42 x 12 mm — undercarriage (bogies)
Two 75 x 42 x 12 mm — undercarriage (bogies)
250 x 70 x 19 mm — wheels

6 mm dowelling
Two 85 mm lengths — axles
30 mm length — coupling pin

MATERIALS
Four 6 mm screw eyes
20 mm bullet head nails

EQUIPMENT
6 mm drill bit
8 mm drill bit
50 mm hole saw

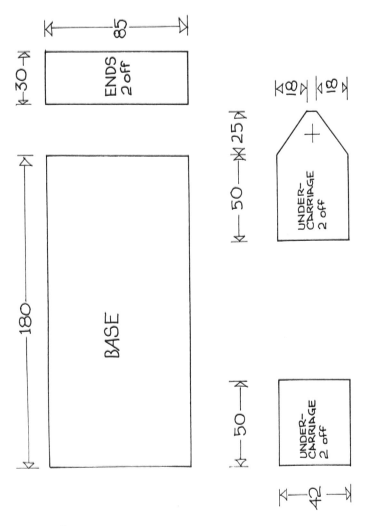

ENDS
2 off

85

30

BASE

180

UNDER-
CARRIAGE
2 off

18

18

50

25

50

UNDER-
CARRIAGE
2 off

42

INSTRUCTIONS

1. Read through all the instructions. Check the template and assembly chart and photograph before beginning the project. Use a photocopier to enlarge the template to full size. Trace the template diagrams onto the pieces of wood listed in the cutting list.

2. Cut the base and the two ends.

3. Using 20 mm bullet head nails, glue and nail the ends to the base, flush with the ends.

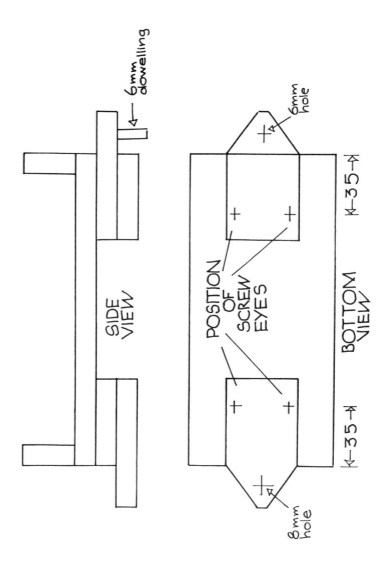

SIDE VIEW

6mm dowelling

POSITION OF SCREW EYES

BOTTOM VIEW

6mm hole

8mm hole

35

35

4. Cut the two 50 mm blocks and the two tapered ends of the undercarriage (bogies). Drill a 6 mm hole in one tapered end and a 8 mm hole in the other, as marked on the template.

5. To the underside of the base, glue and nail one of the undercarriage blocks to one end centred and flush, with the end. To the other end of the base glue and nail one of the tapered lengths (with the 6 mm hole). Make sure the tapered length extends 25 mm from the end of the base.

6. Glue the coupling pin into the 6 mm hole making sure the dowelling is protruding down. On to this assembly glue the other 50 mm block in the position shown on the template.

7. Glue and nail the other tapered length (with the 8 mm hole) to the 50 mm block already assembled at the other end of base. Make sure that the tapered length extends 25 mm from the end of the base.

8. Using a 50 mm hole saw, cut four wheels. Sand and paint the wheels and the base assembly, separately.

9. Attach screw eyes to the assembled undercarriage in the position shown in the assembly chart. Pass the axles through screw eyes and glue on the wheels.

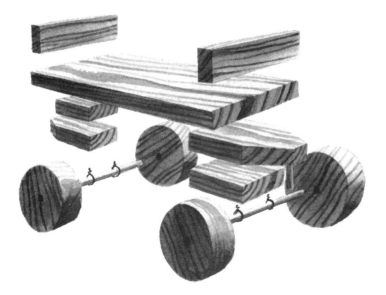

Train
Box car

CUTTING LIST

Pine
Two 180 x 85 x 12 mm — top and base
Two 70 x 85 x 12 mm — ends
Two 50 x 42 x 12 mm — undercarriage
Two 75 x 42 x 12 mm — undercarriage
wheels as for flat car

4 mm plywood
Four pieces 94 x 60 mm — sides

6 mm dowelling
Two lengths to 85 mm — axles
One length to 30 mm — coupling pin

MATERIALS
6 mm screw eyes
20 mm bullet head nails

EQUIPMENT
6 mm drill bit
8 mm drill bit
50 mm hole saw

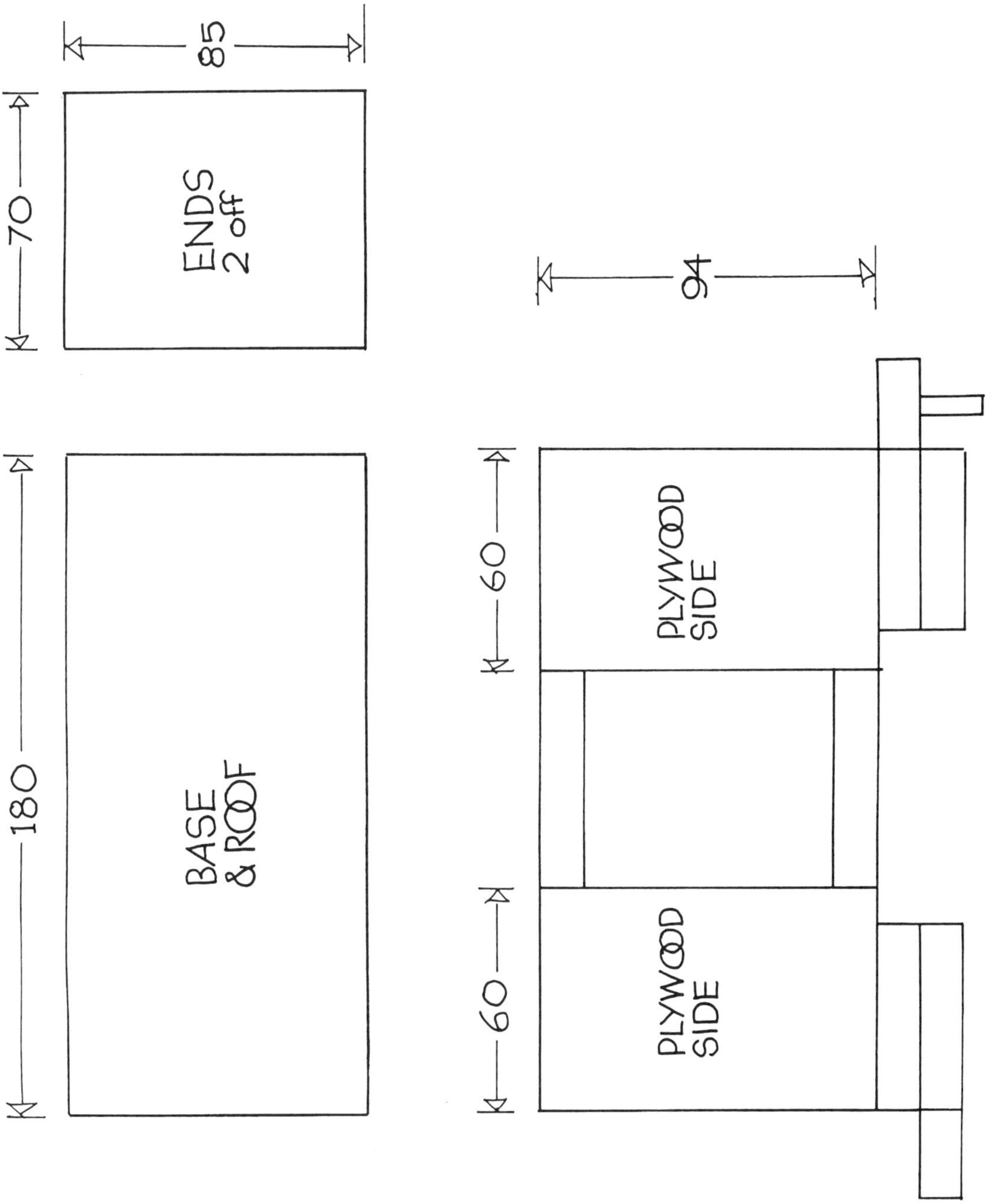

85

70

ENDS
2 off

180

BASE
& ROOF

94

60

PLYWOOD
SIDE

60

PLYWOOD
SIDE

INSTRUCTIONS

1. Read through all the instructions. Check the template and assembly chart and photograph before beginning the project. Use a photocopier to enlarge the template to full size. Trace the template diagrams onto the pieces of wood listed in the cutting list.

2. Cut out the top, base, and ends. Glue and nail together, as shown.

3. Cut out the sides. Glue and nail to the sides, flush with the ends but leaving an opening in the middle of each side.

4. Cut and assemble undercarriage as per the instructions for the Flat Car.

Helicopter

CUTTING LIST

Pine

300 x 120 x 12 mm — two side panels of cockpit

22 x 42 x 12 mm — cockpit front

128 x 42 x 12 mm — cockpit floor

95 x 42 x 35 mm — rotor support

60 x 45 x 19 mm — side span support block and side span spreader block

4 mm plywood

Two 149 x 45 mm — side spans

280 x 20 mm — rotor

60 x 12 mm — rear propeller

66 x 82 mm — cockpit roof

12 mm square moulding

Two lengths 140 mm — landing skids

Two lengths 105 mm — skid supports

6 mm dowelling

Two 20 mm lengths

MATERIALS

Two 15 mm 6 gauge round head screws

Four washers to fit round head screws

40 mm bullet head nails

12 mm bullet head nails

20 mm bullet head nails

25 mm flat head nails

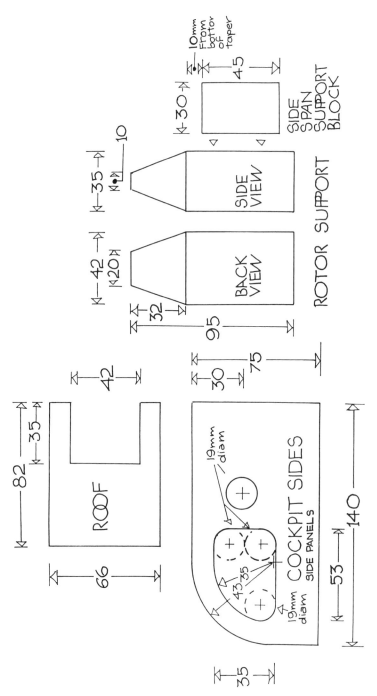

10mm From bottom of taper

30
45

SIDE SPAN SUPPORT BLOCK

35
10

SIDE VIEW

42
20

BACK VIEW

32
95

ROTOR SUPPORT

42

30
75

82
35

66

ROOF

19mm diam

COCKPIT SIDES
SIDE PANELS

43 35

19mm diam

53
140

35

EQUIPMENT

19 mm hole saw

25 mm hole saw

Keyhole saw

6 mm drill bit

8 mm drill bit

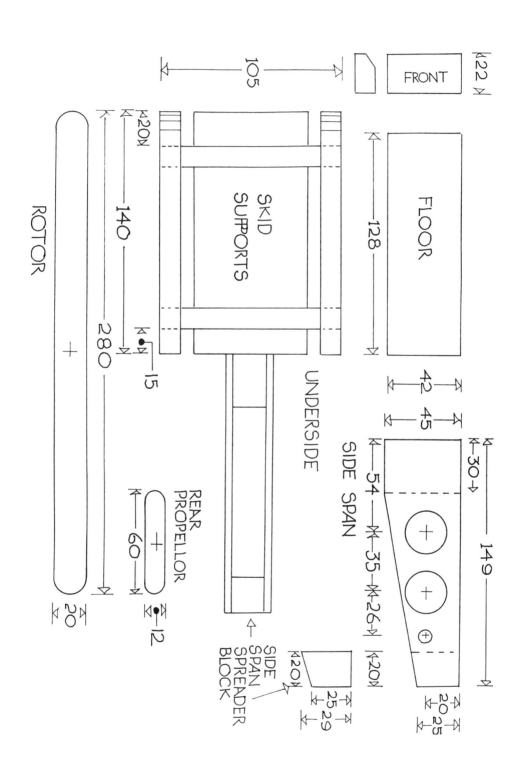

FRONT

105

22

ROTOR

SKID
SUPORTS

FLOOR

128

20

140

280

15

20

UNDERSIDE

REAR
PROPELLOR

60

12

20

SIDE SPAN

42

45

30

149

54

35

26

20

20
25

SIDE
SPAN
SPREADER
BLOCK

20

25
29

INSTRUCTIONS

1. Read through all the instructions. Check the template, assembly chart and photograph before beginning the project. Use a photocopier to enlarge the template to full size. Trace the template diagrams onto the pieces of wood listed in the cutting list.

2. Before cutting out the cockpit sides, cut out the cockpit windows and portholes using a 19 mm hole saw at the corners. Finish cutting the window with a keyhole saw. Then cut out the cockpit sides.

3. Cut out the cockpit floor and the cockpit front. Bevel the cockpit front at the top then glue and nail the cockpit front to the cockpit floor using 20 mm bullet head nails (see diagram B).

4. Cut out the rotor support. Taper one end of the block, as shown in the template.

5. Glue and nail the rotor support flush with the rear end of the cockpit floor using 40 mm bullet head nails (see diagram B).

6. Glue and nail the side panels to the cockpit assembly using 20 mm bullet head nails.

7. Cut out the cockpit roof. Glue and nail the roof into position using 12 mm bullet head nails.

8. Cut out the side span support block and attached it to the rear of the rotor support use dowelling. Drill the 6 mm dowelling holes straight through the side span support block. Line up the holes and mark the corresponding

Attach side span support block to rotor support block using 6 mm dowelling

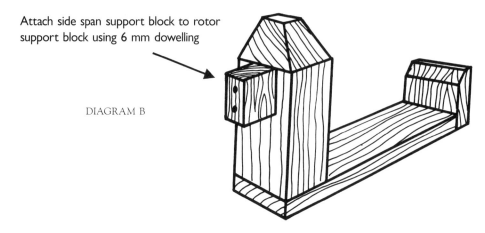

DIAGRAM B

position on the rotor support before drilling the holes in the rotor support (see diagram B).

9. Before cutting out the two side spans, cut the two larger holes using a 25 mm hole saw. Cut the smaller hole using an 8 mm drill.

10. Glue and nail the side span spreader block between the ends of the side spans using 20 mm bullet head nails. Sand it to fit flush with ends, as shown in the template.

11. Glue and nail this assembly to the side span support block using 12 mm bullet head nails. Sand off any rough edges.

12. Using the template as a guide, round off the front ends of each of the undercarriage skids. Glue and nail the undercarriage skids to the skid supports using 20 mm bullet head nails. Glue and nail this assembly to the bottom of the cockpit floor using 25 mm bullet head nails.

13. Cut out the rotor and rear propeller. Drill holes in the centre of the rotor and the propeller to accommodate the screws.

14. Attach the rotor to its support block using a 15 mm round head screw and washers to fit. Attach the rear propeller to the left hand side span so that the screw enters the rear spreader. Use a 15 mm round head screw and washers to fit. Make sure the rotor and propeller can spin freely.

15. Paint or varnish.

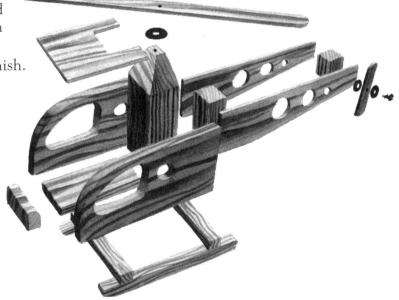

Sewing machine

CUTTING LIST

Pine

200 x 90 x 35 mm — base
128 x 42 x 35 mm — vertical support post
68 x 42 x 35 mm — needle end
420 x 140 x 12 mm — side panels
152 x 42 x 12 mm — bottom of arm
200 x 42 x 12 mm — top
40 x 42 x 12 mm — shaft support
150 x 70 x 12 mm — operating wheel, shaft wheel, stitch dial, thread tensioner

4 mm plywood

32 mm diameter disc — top of thread tensioner

6 mm dowelling

30 mm length — operating wheel handle
50 mm length — cotton reel holder
20 mm length — stitch dial to front panel
20 mm length — thread tensioner to front panel

8 mm dowelling

200 mm length — shaft

10 mm dowelling

100 mm length — needle

MATERIALS

One 3 mm x 25 mm machine screw
One spring washer
Two nuts to fit the machine screw

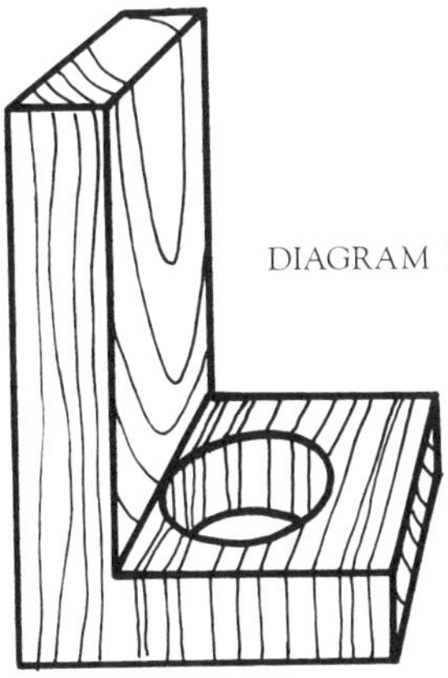

DIAGRAM 1

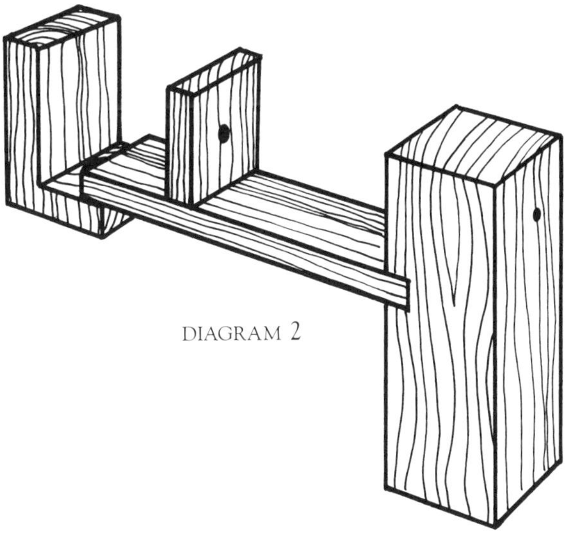

DIAGRAM 2

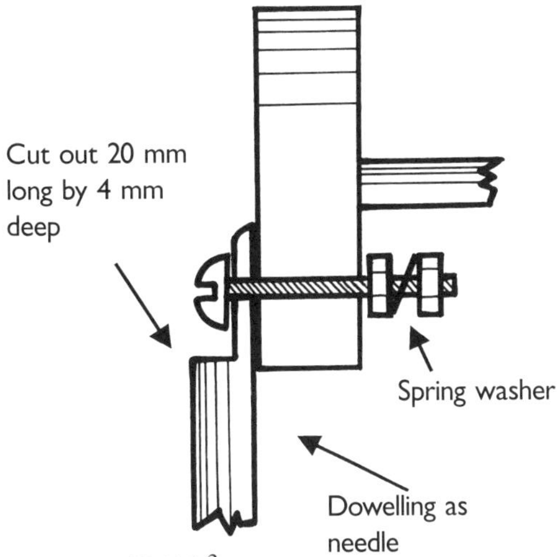

Cut out 20 mm
long by 4 mm
deep

Spring washer

Dowelling as
needle

DIAGRAM 3

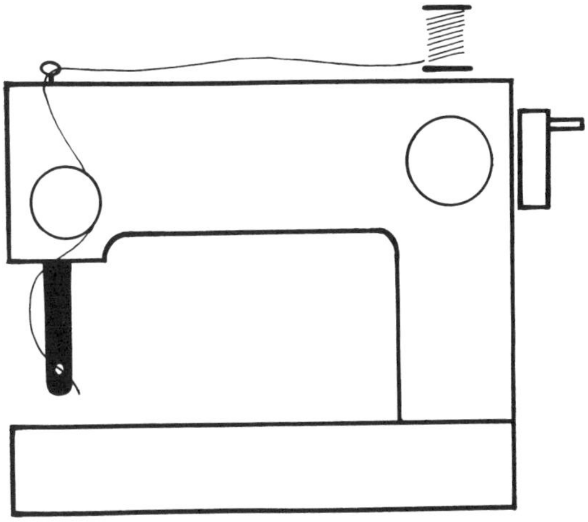

DIAGRAM 4

Eight 6 gauge x 25 mm long screws
10 mm washer
Two 8 gauge x 50 mm screws
20 mm bullet head nails
30 mm bullet head nails

EQUIPMENT
3.5 mm drill bit
6 mm drill bit
8 mm drill bit
9 mm drill bit
15 mm spade bit
32 mm hole saw
50 mm hole saw

INSTRUCTIONS

1. Read through all the instructions. Check the template and assembly chart and photograph before beginning the project. Use a photocopier to enlarge the template to full size. Trace the template diagrams onto the pieces of wood listed in the cutting list.

2. Cut the base of the sewing machine. Round off the sharp edges with sandpaper

3. Cut the vertical support post. Into the vertical support post, cut a trench 12 mm wide by 12 mm deep, as shown on the template. Drill a 9 mm hole in the position shown on the template.

4. Cut the needle end to an 'L' shape, as shown in the template. At the base of the 'L' shape drill a 15 mm hole (see diagram 1).

5. Cut the bottom of the arm. Using 20 mm bullet head nails (pre-drill pilot holes) and glue, join the bottom of the arm to the base of the needle end. Fix this assembly into the trench in the vertical support post using glue and 30 mm bullet head nails.

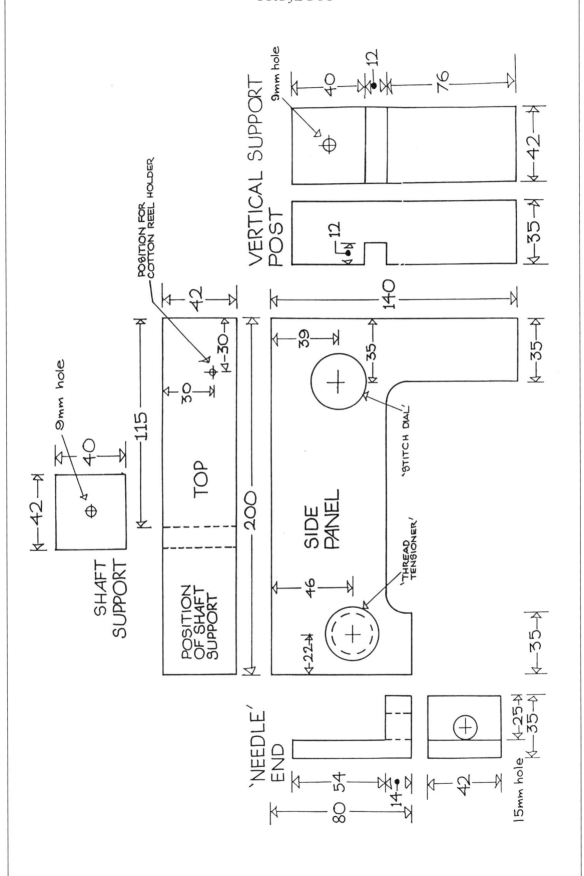

VERTICAL SUPPORT POST

9mm hole

40

12

76

42

35

12

SHAFT SUPPORT

9mm hole

40

42

POSITION FOR COTTON REEL HOLDER

42

TOP

115

30

30

200

POSITION OF SHAFT SUPPORT

SIDE PANEL

140

39

35

'STITCH DIAL'

35

46

'THREAD TENSIONER'

22

35

'NEEDLE' END

80

54

14

42

25

35

15mm hole

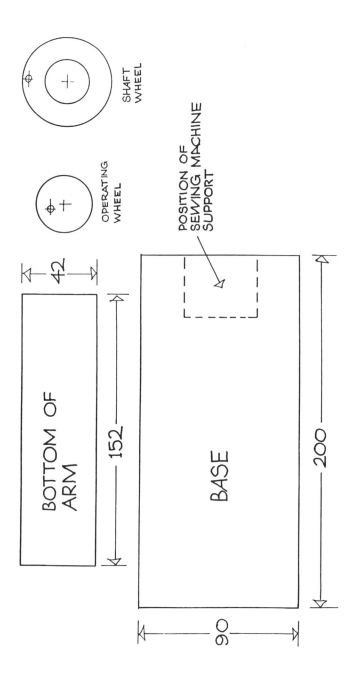

6. Cut out the sewing machine top. Drill a 6 mm hole for the cotton reel holder, as shown on the template. Glue and nail the top to the vertical support post and the top of the needle end using 20 mm bullet head nails.

7. Cut out the shaft support. Drill a 9 mm hole in the centre, as shown in the template. Glue the shaft support into position so that it fits snugly

between the top and bottom of arm, 115 mm from the vertical support arm. Nail the shaft support into position using 20 mm bullet head nails. Punch the heads below the surface and fill the holes.

8. Screw this assembly to the base using two 50 mm x 8 gauge screws fixed from underneath.

9. To cut the operating wheel and create a wheel hub first drill about 6 mm down using a 50 mm diameter hole saw. Remove the hole saw and, using a 25 mm spade bit, line up the centres then drill down about 3 mm. Remove the spade bit and finish drilling out the wheel using the 50 mm hole saw. Enlarge the centre hole to a diameter of 8 mm. Next, drill a 6 mm diameter hole near the rim of the wheel. Glue the operating wheel handle into the rim hole.

10. Pass the shaft through the hole in the vertical support post and the hole in shaft support. Leave some of the shaft protruding from the vertical support post.

11. With a 32 mm diameter hole saw, cut out the shaft wheel. Drill out the centre hole to an 8 mm diameter. Then drill a 3.5 mm hole half way between the centre and the rim.

12. To make the needle, drill a 3.5 mm hole through the dowelling about 10 mm from the end. Shape the end to a rounded point. At the other end of the needle, cut out a piece 20 mm long x 4 mm deep, as shown in the diagram 3. Next, drill a 3.5 mm hole through the cut out section, 10 mm from the end.

13. Glue the 32 mm diameter wheel to the shaft. Place the machine screw in the hole at the top of the needle (the cut out end), then pass the needle down through the hole in the needle end. Fasten the machine screw to the shaft wheel by using the two nuts separated by the spring washer, as shown in diagram 3. Make sure the nut against the wheel is loose enough to let the wheel turn freely. Tighten the outside nut against the spring washer so that it does not undo when the wheel turns.

14. Glue the operating wheel to the shaft protruding from the hole in the vertical

support post. Separate the wheel from the post with a 10 mm washer.

15. The thread tensioner is made up of a 25mm diameter wheel and a 32 mm diameter disc of plywood glued and nailed together (using 12 mm bullet head nails), centre holes matching.

16. Cut out the stitch dial using a 32 mm hole saw. Cut out the side panels. Drill 6 mm holes through the side panels in the positions marked on the template for the thread tensioner and the stitch dial. Use 6 mm dowelling to attach the thread tensioner and stitch dial to the side panels.

17. Screw the side panels to the assembled machine using eight (four for the front and four for the back) 25 mm 6 gauge countersunk screws in pre-drilled pilot holes. DO NOT GLUE THE PANELS TO THE MACHINE. This will enable access to the interior if the moving parts get stuck or broken.

18. Attach the cotton reel holder to the hole in the top of the machine. Sand off the sharp edges and paint the sewing machine, making sure the moving parts are able to move freely.

19. Screw a 6 mm screw eye onto the top side panel above the thread tensioner. Get an old cotton reel, wind on some string and pass the string through the screw eye, loop the string around the thread tensioner and through the hole in the needle. See diagram 4.

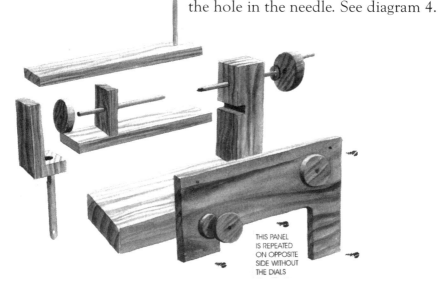

THIS PANEL IS REPEATED ON OPPOSITE SIDE WITHOUT THE DIALS